Endeavor

③ ------- Teacher's
Guide

New Readers Press
A Publishing Division of ProLiteracy

Endeavor 3: Teacher's Guide
ISBN 978-1-56420-871-2

Copyright © 2009 New Readers Press
New Readers Press
A Publishing Division of ProLiteracy
1320 Jamesville Avenue, Syracuse, New York 13210
www.newreaderspress.com

Printed in the United States of America
9 8 7 6 5 4 3 2

All proceeds from the sale of New Readers Press materials support literacy programs in the United States and worldwide.

Contributing Author: Vista Resources, Inc.
Developmental Editors: Ellen Northcutt, Donna Townsend
Creative Director: Andrea Woodbury
Production Specialist: Maryellen Casey

Contents

Strategies for Success with *Endeavor*

Tips for Planning Instruction

There are a number of strategies that you can implement to maximize the effectiveness of *Endeavor's* lesson plans. First, always prepare your lessons before class. This includes reading and practicing the text of the story, selecting activities, and preparing materials. Although the *Endeavor* Teacher's Guide is intended to provide ideas and guidance, it is not meant as a script. Use the explanations in the Teacher's Guide to help you develop explanations in your own words. Additionally, modify the questions, examples, and activities to suit the needs of your students. If, for example, some students need more time to complete an element in the lesson, determine which activities you can omit or shortcut in order for students to have the time they need to be successful. Remember, the objective is for students to feel satisfaction as they become aware of their gains in building reading, writing, and other language skills.

Tips for Implementing Instruction

Students should be clear about what is expected of them. Therefore, inform students of the learning goals and outcomes before beginning a lesson. This Teacher's Guide provides learning objectives on the first page of notes for each lesson. Students should also be clear about how they will perform the tasks required of them. It is imperative, therefore, that you model every new skill, and model skills again if your students have not practiced them in a while. For example, model a sentence that uses a new vocabulary word correctly and in a meaningful context, and then work with students to explain what made your sentence effective. This kind of explicit skill modeling will make your expectations clear to your students. Students will begin to internalize what constitutes a complete answer or a meaningful interaction with a text.

In addition to modeling skills, you will also want to model strategies. Create your own Think About Its to complement those incorporated in the student book. Modeling how you think as you read will provide students with concrete examples of the ways that they should be interacting with text. If you realize that your students have never taken notes as they read, model notetaking. Use a text photocopied onto an overhead transparency and demonstrate how you highlight relevant passages or take notes on the side of the text. The more specific you are and the more examples you give of the various skills and strategies, the clearer the understanding will be in students' minds. Use of the active reading strategies should become second nature to students. This will occur with repetition, so remind them to use strategies that they have already learned.

Fluency and vocabulary development are important components of your students' reading growth. Therefore, you and your students should read aloud whenever possible. Not only will students get to listen to your fluent model and practice their own oral fluency, but students' reading will provide an opportunity for you to do informal assessments. Similarly, the Vocabulary Knowledge Rating Chart (Master 9) can help you to assess your students' facility with words and can inform your vocabulary instruction. If, for instance, most of your students indicate that they fully understand the word *bruised*, but the word *permeated* is unfamiliar, spend your instructional time on the unfamiliar word. Additionally, spend more time on the words that students are likely to encounter in a variety of texts—the key vocabulary words—rather than specialized vocabulary. There are activities and suggestions throughout the Teacher's Guide to assist you in your explanations and planning.

Tips for Maximizing Students as Resources

The life experience of adult learners is invaluable, so make sure that you are bringing students' prior knowledge into every aspect of your teaching. Make your examples relevant to students' experience, and allow them to draw connections between what they are learning and what they already know. The stories and articles in *Endeavor* were selected because they are likely in some way to relate to students' life experiences and concerns. Find those connections, and make them clear to students.

In addition to utilizing students' prior knowledge in your lessons, use students as resources for themselves and one another. The Revising and Editing Checklist (Master 11) is provided as a tool for students. They can check and improve their own and their peers' work using very specific criteria. As always, model the use of the Revising and Editing Checklist, and give students ample opportunity to practice with it. Also, have students use the Writing Rubric (Master 10) to evaluate their completed pieces against measures of ideas, organization, voice, and conventions. Compare your evaluations with theirs as part of writing conferences. These strategies for self- and peer-evaluation do not preclude the need for teacher assessment, but they do give students another set of eyes as they review their own work. The Revising and Editing Checklist and the Writing Rubric allow students to work with and eventually internalize criteria for an acceptable piece of writing.

Assessment is the key to determining if your instruction has been successful and if your students are progressing. You should be using periodic formal assessments, such as the TABE (Tests of Adult Basic Education) or another instrument, to track your students' progress. Informal assessments are important as well, particularly when it comes to modifying your instruction from lesson to lesson. Informal assessments include checklists of skills, over-the-shoulder analyses of students' reading, and your evaluations of students' class work. Although *Endeavor* provides rich resources in terms of texts, activities, strategies, and pedagogy, ultimately it is you, the teacher, who is most important to your students' success. It is your preparation, modeling, and evaluation that will ensure that your students are growing as learners, readers, and writers. We welcome you and wish you luck as you embark on this *Endeavor*.

Suggestions for Developing Vocabulary

Key Vocabulary

The key vocabulary words have been chosen because they are likely to be entirely unfamiliar or somewhat unfamiliar to many students. By working with these words before students begin reading, you are giving students additional keys with which to unlock the meaning of the text. The more they know before reading, the more they are likely to take with them from the reading.

In addition to helping students comprehend a particular text, vocabulary study will provide students with new words to add to their working vocabularies. As their vocabularies grow, they will be able to read increasingly more complex texts. They will also be able to express themselves in a more sophisticated manner in their writing and speaking.

Side-Column Vocabulary

Vocabulary words can be broken down into three tiers. Tier 1 words are the most basic words. These words (like *shoe, paper,* and *sad*) do not need to be taught, because they are already part of students' vocabularies. Tier 2 words (like *schedule, ceremony,* and *exhausted*) are found in more sophisticated texts and across a variety of domains. These are the kinds of words that have been selected as key vocabulary words.

Tier 3 words (like *insomnia, ancestors,* and *chlorine*) are specialized vocabulary. These words appear infrequently in texts and generally apply only to specific domains. These are the kinds of words that have been selected as side-column vocabulary. Although it will be useful to teach these words in the context of the particular text you are reading, they are not likely to appear frequently or in a variety of texts. Therefore, *Endeavor* focuses more on direct instruction and practice of Tier 2 words than it does on Tier 3 words.

How to Use the Vocabulary Knowledge Rating Chart

The Vocabulary Knowledge Rating Chart (Master 9) is a quick tool for determining students' prior knowledge of each of the vocabulary words. Not only will it help students focus on each of the words, but it will give you a sense of the words on which you will want to concentrate instruction.

Model the use of the Vocabulary Knowledge Rating Chart when you first introduce it. Once students are familiar with the chart, however, they should be able to use it on subsequent sets of words quickly and without extensive instruction.

Tips for Teaching Vocabulary

- The key to learning vocabulary is practice. Each lesson guide includes a number of different strategies for vocabulary practice. Provide as many opportunities as possible for students to interact with and practice the new words.

- Be sure to reframe students' sentences if they are using words incorrectly, and provide additional examples and explanations if necessary. If students learn vocabulary words incorrectly, they will use them incorrectly in the future.

- Use challenging vocabulary when you are talking to your students. Your modeling will help them use words in appropriate contexts, and the unfamiliar words you use will encourage students to explore vocabulary beyond what is being explicitly taught.

- Encourage students to use their new vocabulary words in their everyday lives, and invite them to share anecdotes of when they use the words or encounter the words in conversations or in the media.

Suggestions for Keeping Personal Dictionaries

Personal dictionaries are meant both as spelling aids and as places to record and explore new vocabulary words. For maximum benefit, personal dictionaries should be user-friendly.

A personal dictionary can be created from a notebook or from paper stapled or bound together. It should be its own entity rather than part of another notebook. This will make it more easily accessible and portable as students move through various levels of *Endeavor*. The personal dictionary should be organized alphabetically and have at least four full pages for each letter, perhaps fewer for the less frequently used letters.

Since vocabulary words are best internalized when they are used often, it is important that personal dictionaries be interactive. Students should enter new words they encounter from their experience and from the texts and other print material they are reading. Ask them to include a clear definition and part of speech along with sentences, examples, sketches, or other means for them to internalize a full, clear meaning of the term. Students should have a voice in deciding what to include in an entry.

Plan frequent activities that require students to return to the words they have recorded. Have students find a "k" word and share it with a neighbor; dramatize a "p" word and have the class guess it; sketch a simple drawing of a word; or write a sentence, correctly using at least three of their vocabulary words. If students simply enter the words and never return to them, the benefit of the personal dictionary will be minimal.

Inside the front and back covers of the personal dictionary, have students record words that are particularly challenging for them to spell. This will limit the number of times they need to search for those words in a large dictionary. It also gives the teacher a place to record words that students are consistently misspelling in their writing. Finally, it ensures that the personal dictionary is being utilized often, as it will be on students' desks as they are writing.

Suggestions for Writing Portfolios

A writing portfolio is intended to hold student work so that the student, teacher, or observer can see how the student has developed as a writer. A portfolio can be a file folder, a box, or a large envelope. Ask each student to create his or her own portfolio. Portfolios can include any writing that the student has done. If the class is producing a lot of work, you will want to pick and choose items for the portfolio so that it doesn't become unmanageable and unusable. Encourage students to include pieces that they are particularly proud of. The goal is to have the contents organized and accessible.

By reviewing their portfolios, students, and particularly adult students, will have the opportunity to evaluate their own work and growth. They will also have access to the teacher's observations and evaluations of their work. Moreover, portfolios might include copies of the Writing Rubric (Master 10) which students can use to evaluate and comment on their own work. Self-evaluations of final drafts of writing can be modeled by the teacher and done often.

Writing portfolios should be interactive rather than stored out of reach. Students use them to review their work and note their progress. In addition, students should have the opportunity to return to a piece they have written, work to improve it, and then publish it in a creative way. By continuing to interact with their writing and evaluating their own progress, students will remain motivated to improve their writing.

Developing Fluency

Fluency is a reader's ability to recognize words automatically and accurately and to read aloud with appropriate expression. The expression is called *prosody*, and it includes intonation, stress, rate, rhythm, and phrasing. Prosody is important to a reader's understanding of the text. Students must comprehend what they are reading in addition to reading quickly and accurately; therefore, teachers must effectively model and teach prosody. And students need repetition in order to develop fluency.

Although the teacher is an important model of fluent reading, the teacher cannot work individually with every student at the same time. Also, in any group of readers, there are likely to be some differences in students' ability to read orally. Therefore, strategies have been developed to help classrooms of readers at different levels to work on fluency simultaneously. These strategies usually include modeling and repetition.

Fluency in *Endeavor*

Endeavor supports you as you work with your students to improve their fluency. Each lesson in the Teacher's Guide provides strategies you can use to practice fluency. With any of the texts, you may wish to use other strategies in addition to those described in the lesson.

Strategies

Echo Reading—With Echo Reading, students imitate fluent reading modeled by the teacher. The teacher reads aloud, and the students are the echo. Depending upon the level of the readers in your class, you will break the

text into phrases or full sentences. Read the phrase or sentence aloud, paying careful attention to your accuracy and prosody. Then have the class repeat the phrase or sentence, also paying careful attention to accuracy and prosody. Continue reading aloud and having the class echo you for the rest of the passage. Be sure to break the text at logical points in order to maintain the meaning of the text.

Choral Reading—Choral Reading involves students reading aloud together, like a chorus. The teacher begins by reading the chosen passage aloud, concentrating on accuracy and prosody. Then students read the same passage aloud in groups ranging from three students to the whole class reading together. In order to set and maintain the pace, the teacher reads aloud with the students. Choral Reading allows readers the opportunity to practice fluency in a situation where they are supported by other readers.

Paired Repeated Reading—Paired Repeated Reading involves students working with one another—rather than one-on-one with the teacher—in order to improve their fluency. Students work in pairs, and each partner selects a passage to read aloud. Students begin by reading their passages silently. Then partners take turns being the reader or listener. Readers read their passages aloud three times. After the first reading, the listener does not provide feedback. After the second and third readings, the listener provides feedback to the reader.

Be sure to explain and model for students how to give one another constructive feedback. Model directly for students, using a volunteer reader. Tell students that comments such as, "I didn't know from your reading that this sentence was a question" or "I could understand you better if you slowed down and read louder" are more helpful than "Good job." Do a *fishbowl* exercise where the class observes a pair of readers and the class gives feedback on the pairs' feedback to one another. Once students are clear on how to give each other feedback, you will not have to repeat the modeling or fishbowl.

Reading to the Teacher—With small numbers of students in a class, it is possible to give regular attention on fluency to individual students. This gives you a clear sense of each student's strengths and weaknesses. Have students choose passages. Give them an opportunity to review them before they read them aloud to you. Give specific and constructive feedback on accuracy and prosody immediately after the reading. You can also use Echo Reading one-on-one to give students the opportunity for repetition.

Popcorn Reading—With popcorn reading, students take turns reading aloud. Students do not know who is going to be reading next, just as you do not know which kernel of corn will pop next. One student reads a sentence, a few sentences, or a paragraph. Then, he or she says "Popcorn, . . ." and calls another student's name. That student reads part of the passage and then *popcorns* someone else. Students stay on their toes, because they do not know who will be reading next.

Performance Reading—Many students enjoy working in pairs or small groups to dramatize the text they are reading. This strategy works well with texts that include a lot of dialogue. Assign students different roles, and have them practice the dialogue for their characters so that they are able to read their parts fluently and with expression from the text. Then have students perform for the class.

Fluency Tips for the Teacher
- Read and prepare the text before coming to class. It is easier to model fluency if you are already familiar with the text.
- Make sure students are familiar with the text before they begin to work on fluency. If students have already worked with the vocabulary and content of

the text, they will struggle less with pronunciation and phrasing.
- You can use different fluency strategies with the same text. On one day, you might choose to use Echo Reading with a particular story; the next day, you might choose a passage from the same story and do Choral Reading. Remember that repetition is one of the keys to enhancing fluency.
- When pairing students, split the class into two groups according to reading ability. Have the top student of your more able readers work with the top student of your less able readers (conversely, have the low student of your best readers work with the lowest student of your lowest readers.) This may minimize frustration while still providing readers with support.

Keeping Track of Students' Progress
You will want to keep track of your students' reading progress. You can do this by informally recording each individual student's reading accuracy.

- Begin by choosing an unfamiliar passage of about 200 words in length that is at the student's reading level (perhaps from the next lesson in his or her student book or from the student books above or below that level.) Have the student read the passage aloud to you.
- On a separate copy of the same text, put a check mark over each word that is properly read. Each time a reader substitutes, omits, or inserts a word, count it as an error. If the student corrects herself, do not count those words as errors.
- Tally the errors and determine the percentage of words that were accurately read.
- Record a student's reading accuracy every few weeks in order to track progress.

Note: Running Records can be used to do a more thorough analysis of a student's reading and enable you to address individual challenges. You can go online to find explanations and examples of Running Records.

Good Sleep for Good Health

Lesson Overview: (PAGE 5)

Theme

Have students read the lesson title on page 5 and tell them that the title introduces the lesson theme, Health. Discuss the theme by having students make personal connections, telling about instances in which they felt healthy or sick and describing what they were feeling.

Learning objectives

Be sure students understand the outcome of each of the learning goals.

- *Learn how to get a good night's sleep.* The article is relevant to everyone because at one time or another, everyone has difficulty getting a good night's rest. Provide background, explaining that this article is nonfiction. It gives facts that are based on research.
- *Learn to identify cause and effect.*
- *Master the key vocabulary used in the article.*
- *Write sentences that tell about a time when you did not sleep well.*

Preteach the vocabulary. (PAGE 5)

Read the key vocabulary words and their definitions to the students. Tell them that they will recognize all these words in the article.

- Distribute the Vocabulary Knowledge Rating Chart (Master 9) and have students individually rate each of the key vocabulary words.
- Preview particularly challenging words with students by listing each one on the board, modeling its use in a sentence, and having two or three students use the word in original sentences. Reframe student sentences that do not use the new words correctly.

You may wish to offer a mini-lesson on verbs as students read the respective parts of speech with the definitions of the vocabulary words. [See page 40 of this book for a mini-lesson on verbs. Use Master 3 or 4 to give students practice in recognizing verbs.]

Before You Read (PAGE 6)

Explain that active readers get more out of their reading. They respond to what they read, and that helps them understand the selection better. Active readers may choose one or several strategies. One is to consider what they already know about the topic. As they read, they constantly make connections between their own experiences and what they are reading. Another is to set a purpose for their reading. In other words, they think about what they want to learn from their reading. People who have a purpose for reading find that they remember more.

As students begin to write answers to the questions for each element on page 6, have them read the respective Think About Its.

Use what you know. Use the first Think About It to elicit discussion about what students already know about the causes of insomnia and some solutions. In answering the questions, many students are likely to discuss things that cause sleep problems, such as over-thinking or noise.

Set a purpose for reading. Have students read the title "Getting a Good Night's Sleep" and discuss what the title means. Talk about times when students didn't sleep well. How did students feel the next day? How did that affect their interactions with others? Ask them to think how the article might help them.

Reading the Article (PAGES 7–9)

Emphasize to students that reading to find out the causes and effects of insomnia gives them a purpose for reading the article. It will make them active readers. Underlining main ideas and starring details will keep them involved in the article.

Side-Column Vocabulary Remind students that the vocabulary words and phrases in the side column have been selected as important to the theme and content of the story. These words may be useful in the context of sleep and sleep problems, but they are not necessarily part of everyday language.

Mid-Passage Questions The answers to the questions are largely students' opinions, so there are not many right or wrong answers. Review students' written answers to assess whether they are getting meaning from the text. They should indicate in their answers that stress is a major cause of people's sleep problems. Students should also mention that it's important to get to sleep at the same time each night so that the body is used to a regular schedule.

After You Read (PAGES 10–11)

Build a robust vocabulary. Ask students to check their answers in the answer keys in their books.

Think about your reading. Ask students to check their answers in the answer keys in their books. Ask additional questions to enrich the discussion so that students will be better able to write about a time when they did not sleep well. Here are some possible questions:

- Perhaps students have heard the phrases "to sleep like a baby" and "to sleep like a log." Ask *What do the phrases mean? Do you agree or disagree that to sleep like a baby means to sleep well? Have you ever slept like a log?*

- Tell students to imagine that they keep a sleep diary after a night of poor sleep. Ask them what they might write in their diary.

  Extend the reading. Here are some additional activities to expand students' understanding.

  - Ask students to imagine that they work at a sleep clinic. Have them create a booklet with tips called "Three Ways to a Better Night's Sleep."
  - *For English Language Learners* Have students illustrate a wide-awake person lying in bed "counting sheep." Explain that counting sheep is a way that a person who can't sleep visualizes

something in order to banish thoughts that keep her awake. Point out that the counting puts the person into a sleep rhythm. Have students share their illustrations, then add this phrase to their personal dictionaries.

- Ask students to discuss how weather causes people to dress in certain ways. Draw on the board a chart like the one on page 13, and have small groups record types of weather (rain, snow) in the Cause column and how people dress for it in the Effect column (carry an umbrella, wear boots). Have groups discuss and compare their charts.

- Point out to students that this story discusses causes and their effects. Ask students to write down the effect various noises have on someone at home. For example, a phone ringing wakes you up because you have to get up and answer it. Invite students to bring their notes to class and discuss.

Use reading skills: Identify cause and effect. Understanding the causes and effects of behavior or events deepens students' ability to understand relationships between different things and to better understand what they read. Point out that analyzing cause and effect helps in the real world as well. If a worker often comes to work late (the cause), the supervisor might fire him or her or promote someone else (the effect).

Use a graphic organizer. A cause and effect chart can help students understand how information in the article is organized, and can serve as a planning tool to organize a writer's thinking about a text. In this case, the chart visually organizes four measures that affect one's sleep.

Write About It (PAGES 13–14)

Write about a time when you had trouble falling asleep. Have students read the directions on page 13. Be sure they understand that they will write five sentences describing a time they did not sleep well.

Prewriting Have students think about a time when they had a sleep problem. Then ask them to discuss what caused the insomnia and what the effect was. Tell them that these are the types of ideas that they will write in their graphic organizers.

Thinking Beyond Reading   Have students work with a partner or a small group to discuss the questions. The intent is for students to imagine themselves wide-awake at night. How did it make them feel, what did they do to try to fall back asleep, and what, if anything, finally worked to put them back to sleep? Encourage them to add ideas to their cause and effect charts.

Write your sentences.   Have students write five sentences independently. While drafting, students should not be concerned with spelling or punctuation. Encourage them to write their sentences quickly and freely.

Revise and edit.   Remind students to use the Revising and Editing Checklist (Master 11) to guide them in revising their sentences. Have students review each other's sentences and give each other feedback, telling whether the sentences are logical, clear, and interesting. Have them check for capital letters, correct spelling, and punctuation.

When students have finished revising their writing, use the Writing Rubric (Master 10) to evaluate their sentences. Be sure you review the sentences with each student so he or she understands the strengths and weaknesses of this piece of writing. Have students date the writing and put it in their writing portfolios.

Building Fluency

Identify small sections from "Good Sleep for Good Health." Tell students that they will use paired reading to read these sections aloud. Put students into groups of two. Give them time to read a passage silently 2–3 times to encourage their best oral reading. Partners take turns being the reader or listener. After the first reading, the listener does not provide feedback. After the second and third readings, the listener provides feedback to the reader. Remind students to pay attention to words that cause them to stumble and to read for the author's message. Their goal is to read the passage as fluently as if they were just speaking.

A New Way to Work

Lesson Overview: (PAGE 15)

Theme

Have students read the lesson title on page 15 and tell them that the title introduces the lesson theme, Work. Discuss the theme by having students make personal connections, describing jobs they or relatives have had, experiences on the job, and issues related to work, such as pay and working conditions.

Learning Objectives

Be sure students understand the outcome of each of the learning goals.

- *Learn how assembly lines changed the way work is done.* Explain that this article is nonfiction. It tells about real people and events.
- *Learn to classify information.*
- *Master the key vocabulary used in the article.*
- *Write sentences about working on Henry Ford's assembly lines.*

Preteach the vocabulary. (PAGE 15)

Read the key vocabulary words and their definitions to the students. Tell them that they will recognize all these words in the article.

- Distribute the Vocabulary Knowledge Rating Chart (Master 9) and have students individually rate each of the key vocabulary words.
- Preview particularly challenging words with students by listing each one on the board, modeling its use in a sentence, and having two or three students use the word in original sentences. Reframe student sentences that do not use the new words correctly.

You may wish to offer a mini-lesson on nouns as students read the respective parts of speech with the definitions of the vocabulary words. [See page 39 of this book for a mini-lesson on nouns. Use Master 1 or 2 to give students practice in recognizing nouns.]

Before You Read (PAGE 16)

Explain to students that people who are active readers get more out of their reading. They ask questions as they read, and that helps them to understand the selection better. Active readers may choose one or several strategies. They often preview the reading selection, looking at the title, pictures, and headings to see what the article is about. As they read, they constantly make connections between their own prior knowledge and the passage they are reading. What do they know about Henry Ford? What contributions did he make to the automobile industry? They may also classify ideas. For example, if they read about the way cars are produced, they may say to themselves, "This paragraph is about then; that paragraph is about *now*."

As students begin to write answers to the questions for each element on page 16, have them read the respective Think About Its in the side column.

Use what you know. Use the first Think About It about people working in car factories to discuss how students think cars are manufactured. In answering the questions, many students are likely to discuss their own cars, and how they believe cars are assembled.

Ask yourself questions. Explain that the article will be about a man who changed the way people at a car factory did their jobs. Tell them to read to find out what he did that was different. Ask them if they know what an assembly line is and if they have any experience with one. Have them read to find out how Henry Ford was connected to the concept of the assembly line.

Reading the Article (PAGES 17–19)

Emphasize to students that reading to find out what was unusual about Henry Ford's factory gives them a purpose for reading the passage. Underlining main ideas and starring the details will keep them involved in the article.

Side-Column Vocabulary   Remind students that the vocabulary words and phrases in the side column have been selected as important to the theme and content of the story. These words may be useful in the context of working at a factory, but they are not necessarily part of everyday language.

Mid-Passage Questions   The answers to some questions are largely students' opinions, so there are not many right or wrong answers. Review students' written answers to assess whether they are getting meaning from the text. They should indicate in their answers that working at Ford's factory was a good job because workers got good salaries, higher than at other factories. Students should be able to point out that Ford changed the way factory work was done by using an assembly line, and some workers could be unskilled, rather than skilled.

After You Read (PAGES 20–21)

Build a robust vocabulary.   Ask students to check their answers in the answer keys in their books.

Think about your reading.   Ask students to check their answers in the answer keys in their books. Ask additional questions to enrich the discussion so that students will be better able to write about the experience of working on Ford's assembly line. Here are some possible questions:

- A good reader interacts with the text by imagining himself in the article. The article says that there were advantages to workers on Ford's assembly line and doing only one task. Picture yourself as a worker there. What are some disadvantages of doing only one task all day long? How might that affect your interest in the job?

- Ford was innovative, but he could not foresee future changes in factories. Imagine that Henry Ford is alive today. What are some modern techniques that would impress Henry Ford?

  Extend the reading.   Here are some additional activities to expand students' understanding.

  - Ask students to imagine that Henry Ford is being interviewed on radio. He is explaining how his car factory differs from those of the

past. Have students work in pairs, one taking the role of the interviewer, the other, Ford. Have them perform a question and answer interview for other groups, using vocabulary words from the article.

- *For English Language Learners*   Have students reread the next-to-the-last sentence, "New factories *run* fast." Point that that the word *run* has many meanings. Discuss its meaning here, that is, *run* means how it operates or functions. Ask students to give other meanings, for example (1) to ravel, as in She got a *run* in her pantyhose or (2) to go fast, as in They *run* around the track.

- Have students create original sentences, using other meanings of the word *run*. Ask students to add this word to their personal dictionaries.

- Give students additional practice in classifying information. First, have students make a master list on the board of jobs they know, such as schoolteacher, bartender, disc jockey, and bank teller. Ask students to classify these as Day Jobs or Night Jobs. Draw on the board a two-column chart like the one on page 22, and have small groups of students discuss what the job entails and when it's usually performed. Have the groups discuss and compare their charts.

- At home, have each student find a picture of an automobile. Tell them to bring it to class, and to label the parts of the car as to when in the process they were probably put on at the factory, Early or Late. For example, the body parts probably go on *early*, but the tires, lights, bumper, and wipers probably go on *late*.

Use reading skills: Classify information.   Remind students that it is important to be able to classify words and ideas into categories. We constantly apply this thinking skill in our everyday lives. For example, if a person is wondering where to find rolls in a grocery store, he looks at the overhead signs and finds the bread aisle. He is classifying rolls as a kind of bread. Ask students to evaluate whether the assembly line belongs in a list of important innovations in manufacturing. Ask students to classify whether Henry Ford belongs in lists of important

Americans. Point out that students should have reasons for each answer they give.

Use a graphic organizer. The classification chart visually organizes two kinds of workers. Graphic organizers help the reader understand and retain information from the article.

Write About It (PAGES 23–24)

Write sentences about working in Henry Ford's factory. Have students read the directions on page 23. Be sure they understand that they will write five sentences describing the experience of working on Henry Ford's assembly line.

Prewriting Have students think about what it would be like to work at Ford's factory. Then ask them to discuss what a factory worker in Ford's time did on the job, such as install the driver's seat or mount the tires. Ask them to think about how they would feel about that work. Tell them that these are the types of ideas that they will write in their graphic organizers.

Thinking Beyond Reading Have students work with a partner or a small group to discuss the questions. The intent is for students to imagine themselves on the assembly line and to explore issues not mentioned in the article, such as how it feels to work at the factory and their relationships with other workers.

Write your sentences. Have students write five sentences independently. While drafting, students should not be concerned with spelling or punctuation. Encourage them to write their sentences quickly and freely.

Revise and edit. Remind students to use the Revising and Editing Checklist (Master 11) to guide them in revising their sentences. Have students review each other's sentences and give each other feedback, telling whether the sentences are logical, clear, and interesting. Have them check for capital letters, correct spelling, and punctuation.

When students have finished revising their writing, use the Writing Rubric (Master 10) to evaluate their writing. Be sure you review your response with each student so he or she understands the strengths and weaknesses of this piece of writing. Have students date the writing and put it in their writing portfolios.

Building Fluency

Identify small sections from "A New Way to Work." Tell students that they will use paired reading to read these sections aloud. Put students into groups of two. Give them time to read a passage silently 2–3 times to encourage their best oral reading. Partners take turns being the reader or listener. After the first reading, the listener does not provide feedback. After the second and third readings, the listener provides feedback to the reader. Remind students to pay attention to words that cause them to stumble and to read for the author's message. Their goal is to read the passage as fluently as if they were just speaking.

A Family Visit

Lesson Overview: (PAGE 25)

Theme

Have students read the lesson title on page 25 and tell them that the title introduces the lesson theme, Family. Discuss the theme by having students make personal connections, describing family members with whom they are close and ways family members relate to each other.

Learning objectives

Be sure students understand the outcome of each of the learning goals.

- *Read a story about relatives coming to stay with a family.* Point out that this story is fictional. It has characters who are not real, but their problems are like those of people whom we all know.

- *Learn to make judgments.*

- *Master the key vocabulary used in the story.*

- *Write sentences that tell about a time when relatives stayed with you.*

Preteach the vocabulary. (PAGE 25)

Read the key vocabulary words and their definitions to the students. Tell them that they will recognize all these words in the story.

- Distribute the Vocabulary Knowledge Rating Chart (Master 9) and have students individually rate each of the key vocabulary words.

- Preview particularly challenging words with students by listing each one on the board, modeling its use in a sentence, and having two or three students use the word in original sentences. Reframe student sentences that do not use the new words correctly.

You may wish to offer a mini-lesson on adverbs as students read the respective parts of speech with the definitions of the vocabulary words. [See page 42 of this book for a mini-lesson on adverbs. Use Master 7 or 8 to give students practice in recognizing adverbs.]

Before You Read (PAGE 26)

Explain that active readers get more out of reading by responding to ideas or characters in the story. Point out that when good readers read fiction, they might predict what will happen and then check to see if they were right. They might make their own judgments about the characters' decisions.

Tell students, also, that they should develop the habit of reading with a pencil and sticky notes or a small notebook available. They will find that it is always helpful to highlight, underline, and write responses or questions as they read. An involved reader goes back to review his or her notes and marks.

As students begin to write answers to the questions for each element on page 26, have them read the respective Think About Its.

Use what you know. Have students read the title "The Cousins Come to Stay" and discuss what the title means. Use the Think About It to elicit discussion about times when students or people they know have opened their homes to relatives. Encourage students to recall details about times when they may have lived with a relative, how long the stay lasted, and how it worked out.

Make predictions as you read. Talk about how various family members may react to cousins living in their apartment, the advantages and disadvantages of relatives moving in, and issues that may come up when relatives share living space. Ask students to predict whether they think this story will have a happy ending or a sad one. Have them give reasons for their opinions from their own experiences.

Reading the Story (PAGES 27–29)

Emphasize to students that reading to find out if the relatives get along in a crowded apartment gives them a purpose for reading the story. Suggest that they use a highlighter or pencil to mark sentences that show both good feelings and bad feelings. Remind them that they are always looking for clues as to how the story will end.

Side-Column Vocabulary Remind students that the vocabulary words and phrases in the side column have been selected as important to the theme and content of the story. These words may be useful in the context of emotions and family relationships, but they are not necessarily part of everyday language.

Mid-Passage Questions The answers to the questions are largely students' opinions, so there are not many right or wrong answers. Review students' written answers to assess whether they are getting meaning from the text. Answers should indicate what Jackie will do next and how she will behave on the morning of the cousins' arrival. Students should be able to point out that Jackie would be gracious yet rushed when she picks up her cousins at the airport.

After You Read (PAGES 30–31)

Build a robust vocabulary. Ask students to check their answers in the answer keys in their books.

Think about your reading. Ask students to check their answers in the answer keys in their books. Ask additional questions to enrich the discussion so that students will be better able to write about an experience when relatives visited or stayed with them for a while. Here are some possible questions:

- A good reader interacts with the text by imagining him or herself in the story. If you were the cousins, would you have wanted to stay at Jackie's house? What are some advantages and disadvantages? Once they set up their own household, how do you think Juan and Marisol would feel if other cousins from Puerto Rico stayed with them? Would you feel the same way?

- Besides cooking, what are some other ways Juan and Marisol could have helped out in Jackie's house? Do you think those measures would have eased the tension in the household? Why or why not?

Extend the reading. Here are some additional activities to expand students' understanding.

- Ask students to imagine that the weekend has come. Jackie, Lizette and the cousins spend the day together. Based on what students know about the family, how might they pass the time? Sightseeing? Cooking? Playing games? Have students write a few sentences telling what the family did together.

- *For English Language Learners* Have students reread the sentence on page 28 that contains the phrase "made up her mind." Explain that this phrase means "made a decision." Have students use the phrase in a sentence and tell some ways in which they have made up their minds. For example, they may have made up their minds to go back to school or to buy a new car. Ask students to add this phrase to their personal dictionaries.

- Give students additional practice in making judgments about characters' words or actions. On the board, list some things the characters said or did, such as Lola saying *Mom, I'm not sleeping on the couch!* Read the list and discuss whether students agree or disagree with the character's words or behavior. Have students explain their responses.

- At home, have students find recipes for dishes typically eaten in Puerto Rico. They can be main meals, such as rice and beans (*arroz y habichuelas*), or desserts, such as flan. Share recipes.

Use reading skills: Make judgments. Point out that making judgments helps us navigate through our daily lives. When the grocer gives you too much change, do you return the difference? If a fellow student cheats on a test, do you bring it to the attention of the teacher? Explain to students that they can use their prior knowledge and experience to make judgments about a character's words and actions.

Was it kind of Lizette to suggest that the cousins live in a hotel? Did Jackie make the right decision to put up her cousins in their cramped apartment? Posing questions like these not only makes for a spirited discussion but keeps readers involved with the characters and the plot.

Use a graphic organizer. The graphic organizer on page 32 is a two-column chart that can help students use their own experience and the events from the story to evaluate the character's actions. Using this chart will help students isolate each event so that they develop a focused response to each idea and are better able to make judgments about the characters' behavior.

Write About It (PAGES 33–34)

Write about a time when a relative came to visit or stay with you for a while. Have students read the directions at the top of page 33 and be sure they understand that they will write five sentences describing a time when someone stayed with them.

Prewriting Have students think about what it was like when someone stayed with them. How much space did they have, and how did they handle household chores? Tell them that these are the types of ideas that they will write in their graphic organizers.

Thinking Beyond Reading Have students work with a partner or a small group to discuss the questions. The intent is for students to recall how many people visited them, how the visit changed the usual routines, and how extra work in the home got done. Encourage them to add ideas to their graphic organizers.

Write your sentences. Have students write independently. While drafting, students should not be concerned with spelling or punctuation. Encourage them to write their sentences quickly and freely.

Revise and edit. Remind students to use the Revising and Editing Checklist (Master 11) to guide them in revising their writing. Have students review each other's writing and give each other feedback, telling whether the sentences are logical, clear, and interesting. Have them check for capital letters, correct spelling, and punctuation.

When students have finished revising their writing, use the Writing Rubric (Master 10) to evaluate their writing. Be sure you review your response with each student so he or she understands the strengths and weaknesses of this writing. Have students date the writing and put it in their writing portfolios.

Building Fluency

Identify small sections from "The Cousins Come to Stay." Tell students that they will use choral reading to read these sections aloud. (See page 7 for a description of choral reading.) Give them time to read a passage silently 2–3 times to encourage the best oral reading. In order to set and maintain the pace, read along with the students. Identify words that cause the students to stumble. They will imitate the phrasing and intonation that you model. Remind students to use punctuation and typographic cues to add expression to their reading. Tell them that the goal is to read the passage as fluently as if they were just speaking.

Connecting a Community

Lesson Overview: (PAGE 35)

Theme

Have students read the lesson title on page 35 and tell them that the title introduces the lesson theme, Community. Discuss the theme by having students make personal connections, describing ways they meet people in their community and notable places that attract people in their community.

Learning Objectives

Be sure students understand the outcome of each of the learning goals.

- *Learn about how a community helped an artist paint a bridge.* Provide background explaining that this article is nonfiction. It tells about the real people who were involved in the project, and the reader learns about those people's problems and goals.
- *Learn to draw conclusions.*
- *Master the key vocabulary used in the article.*
- *Write sentences that tell about an object or a place that represents the spirit of community.*

Preteach the vocabulary. (PAGE 35)

Read the key vocabulary words and their definitions to the students. Tell them that they will recognize all these words in the article.

- Distribute the Vocabulary Knowledge Rating Chart (Master 9) and have students individually rate each of the key vocabulary words.
- Preview particularly challenging words with students by listing each one on the board, modeling its use in a sentence, and having two or three students use the word in original sentences. Reframe student sentences that do not use the new words correctly.

You may wish to offer a mini-lesson on adjectives as students read the respective parts of speech with the definitions of the vocabulary words. [See page 41 of this book for a mini-lesson on adjectives. Use Master 5 or 6 to give students practice in recognizing adjectives.]

Before You Read (PAGE 36)

Explain that active readers work to get more out of their reading. One way to think about active reading is that it is like talking back to the page. Readers react to what they read. They get involved. When readers do that, they remember more of what they read.

Good readers consider what they already know about the topic and set a purpose for reading. In other words, they ask themselves what they want to learn from the article. People who ask and answer questions as they read also find they remember more. They also find it helpful to read with a pencil and sticky notes or a small notebook available. Then they can highlight, underline, and write responses or questions as they read.

As students begin to write answers to the questions for each element on page 36, have them read the respective Think About Its.

Use what you know. Use the first Think About It to elicit discussion about what bridges are, what they do, and how there can be different kinds of bridges. If possible, get students to discuss both physical bridges and other kinds of "bridges" that bring people together.

Ask yourself questions. Have students read the title "The Community Bridge" and ask questions the title raises in their minds. Have them talk about what they'd like to find out from the article. Read aloud the first paragraph and talk about the main question artist Cochran had for members of the Frederick community. Explain that the article will be about how the community helped Cochran paint the bridge.

Reading the Story (PAGES 37–39)

Emphasize to students that they are reading to find out how the Community Bridge in Frederick, Maryland, came to be. To keep them involved in the article, suggest that students use a highlighter to mark passages that tell about key events that helped the project move forward.

Side-Column Vocabulary   Remind students that the vocabulary words and phrases in the side column have been selected as important to the theme and content of the story. These words may be useful in the context of work that an artist might do, but they are not necessarily part of everyday language.

Mid-Passage Questions   The answers to the questions are largely students' opinions, so there are not many right or wrong answers. Review students' written answers to assess whether they are getting meaning from the text. Answers should indicate that Cochran wanted everyone in Frederick to answer his question because he wanted to include in his project as many people as possible. Students should point out that people put Cochran's question on signs and posters so that everyone had a chance to participate and be heard.

After You Read (PAGES 40–41)

Build a robust vocabulary.   Ask students to check their answers in the answer keys in their books.

Think about your reading.   Ask students to check their answers in the answer keys in their books. Ask additional questions to enrich the discussion so that students will be better able to write about something that symbolizes the spirit of their community. Here are some possible questions:

- The article says that the mural brought the community together. Give specific examples of how things may have changed in Frederick since the completion of the mural.

- If you lived in Frederick, would you have participated in Cochran's project? Why or why not?

   Extend the reading.   Here are some additional activities to expand students' understanding.

- Ask students to imagine that artist William Cochran is delivering a presentation to the local planning board about his proposed bridge project. Have students deliver the presentation using visuals.

- *For English Language Learners* Check that ELL students understand the sequence of events at the beginning of the article. Read aloud the first two paragraphs of the article, in which Cochran gets an idea to find the right object to represent a spirit of community in Frederick, Maryland. Then distribute three sentence strips and ask students to place them in an order that corresponds to the events in the article. Go over the answers and evaluate students' understanding.

- Give students an opportunity to draw further conclusions by exploring the information at the end of the article. Have students imagine that they own a restaurant in Frederick before the bridge was finished. Have students discuss how the restaurant would change once the bridge was painted. Invite students to use the clues from the story (more people visited the city) and their own ideas about a growing city to describe business and activity at the restaurant.

- At home, have each student find a newspaper article about a successful community project. Tell them to read the article, bring it to class, and explain how the project helped the neighborhood.

Use reading skills: Draw conclusions. Drawing conclusions at the end of the article will require that students consider statements made in the article and apply what they already know. This is important for their critical thinking and understanding. Ask students why Cochran wanted everyone in the community to give ideas for the bridge. Discuss problems that a community in general faces when people don't get along. Do they think that having wide participation from many people would have an effect on the project? Ask students how Frederick might have changed after members of the community united to paint the bridge.

Use a graphic organizer.   The chart visually organizes specific ideas from the article and helps students analyze the text in smaller, manageable parts. The reader can better draw conclusions if he or she breaks the information down as the chart shows.

Write About It (PAGES 43–44)

Write about an object that represents the spirit of your community.   Have students read the directions on page 43 and be sure they understand that they will write five sentences telling about an object that represents the spirit of community.

Prewriting   Have students think about which object best represents the spirit of their community. Then ask them to think of three reasons why that object is fitting. Have them visualize the object and think of why they associate it with the best elements of living in their area. Tell them that these are the types of ideas that they will write in the boxes in their graphic organizers.

Thinking Beyond Reading   Have students work with a partner or a small group to discuss their ideas. The intent is for students to discuss their objects, what the objects mean to them, and why they chose them over others. Ask students whether they think others in their community would agree or disagree with their choices. Encourage them to add ideas to their charts.

Write your sentences. Have students write independently. While drafting, students should not be concerned with spelling or punctuation. Encourage them to write their thoughts quickly and freely.

Revise and edit.   Remind students to use the Revising and Editing Checklist (Master 11) to guide them in revising their writing. Have students review each other's writing and give each other feedback, telling whether the sentences are logical, clear, and interesting. Have them check for capital letters, correct spelling, and punctuation.

When students have finished revising their writing, use the Writing Rubric (Master 10) to evaluate their writing. Be sure you review your response with each student so he or she understands the strengths and weaknesses of this piece of writing. Have students date the writing and put it in their writing portfolios.

Building Fluency

Identify small sections from "The Community Bridge." Tell students that they will use paired reading to read these sections aloud. Put students into groups of two. Give them time to read a passage silently 2–3 times to encourage their best oral reading. Partners take turns being the reader or listener. After the first reading, the listener does not provide feedback. After the second and third readings, the listener provides feedback to the reader. Remind students to pay attention to words that cause them to stumble and to read for the author's message. Their goal is to read the passage as fluently as if they were just speaking.

Sing for Your School

Lesson Overview: (PAGE 45)

Theme

Have students read the lesson title on page 45 and tell them that the title introduces the lesson theme, School and Education. Discuss the theme by having students make personal connections, describing schools they have attended, favorite teachers, and favorite subjects.

Learning objectives

Be sure students understand the outcome of each of the learning goals.

- *Learn about how a group of singers raised money for their school.* Point out that this article is nonfiction. It tells about people who really lived in the 19th century and participated in the events that that are described in the article. The events are true.

- *Learn to identify main idea and details.*

- *Master the key vocabulary used in the article.*

- *Write sentences that tell what it might have been like to see the Fisk Jubilee Singers sing.*

Preteach the vocabulary. (PAGE 45)

Read the key vocabulary words and their definitions to the students. Tell them that they will recognize all these words in the article.

- Distribute the Vocabulary Knowledge Rating Chart (Master 9) and have students individually rate each of the key vocabulary words.

- Preview particularly challenging words with students by listing each one on the board, modeling its use in a sentence, and having two or three students use the word in original sentences. Reframe student sentences that do not use the new words correctly.

You may wish to offer a mini-lesson on adjectives as students read the respective parts of speech with the definitions of the vocabulary words. [See page 41 of this book for a mini-lesson on adjectives. Use Master 5 or 6 to give students practice in recognizing adjectives.]

Before You Read (PAGE 46)

Explain that active readers get more out of their reading by "talking back to the page." They react to what they read. They get involved. They may write notes in the margins as certain ideas become important and have personal meaning. Remind them to think about the headings in bold. Suggest that they are always looking for clues to the main ideas that the author wants them to know. As students read, they can ask themselves, "What is the author's point?"

As students begin to write answers to the questions for each element on page 46, have them read the respective Think About Its.

Use what you know.   Use the Think About It to elicit discussion about what the lives of slaves in America were like. In answering the questions, students might discuss the countries slaves came from and where they lived and worked in this country. Involve students in recalling what they know about Africa and America's South in the 18th and 19th centuries. Have them make comparisons. What do they know about the economy of the American South and why slaves were valuable?

Set a purpose for reading.   Have students read the title "The Fisk Jubilee Singers" and discuss what the title means. Talk about singers they know or see on TV and the types of music they like. Explain that the article is about how a group of black singers in the 19th century raised money for their school.

Reading the Article (PAGES 47–49)

Emphasize to students that reading to find out more about how the Fisk Jubilee Singers saved their school gives them a purpose for reading the article. Using a highlighter to mark key sentences will help keep them involved in the article.

Side-Column Vocabulary Remind students that the vocabulary words and phrases in the side column have been selected as important to the theme and content of the story. These words may be useful in the context of musicians and history, but they are not necessarily part of everyday language.

Mid-Passage Questions   The answers to the questions are largely students' opinions, so there are not many right or wrong answers. Review students' written answers to assess whether they are getting meaning from the text. They should indicate in their answers how unusual the Fisk singers were. They should be able to point out that the singers were determined, they knew songs passed down to them through the generations, and they were the first group to sing traditional slave songs for an audience.

After You Read (PAGES 50–51)

Build a robust vocabulary. Ask students to check their answers in the answer keys in their books.

Think about your reading.   Ask students to check their answers in the answer keys in their books. Ask additional questions to enrich the discussion so that students will be better able to write what it would be like to attend a Fisk Jubilee Singers concert. Here are some possible questions:

- Good readers interact with the text by imagining themselves in the article. The article says that the Fisk Jubilee Singers were able to keep alive the songs of their past. Why is it important to keep one's heritage alive? How does it strengthen your feelings about your own people and about yourself?

- Raising money by putting on concerts was an effective way for the Fisk students to expand their school. How else might they have raised money?

   Extend the reading.   Here are some additional activities to expand students' understanding.

- Ask students to imagine they are one of the Fisk Jubilee Singers. Tell them to select a song that they might have sung and bring in the lyrics. Have them explain the meaning of the words. Encourage other students to discuss the lyrics and sing the song.

- *For English Language Learners*   Have students reread the sentence, "Each concert they gave would help *raise* the money that the school needed." Point out that the word *raise* has many meanings. Discuss its meaning here, that is, to collect. Ask students to name other meanings, for example (1) to look after somebody like a parent, "I was *raised* by my grandmother," or (2) to move something up, "Let's *raise* the board about two feet above the ground." Have students create original sentences, using a variety of meanings for the word. Ask students to add this word to their personal dictionaries.

- Give students additional practice in finding the main idea and supporting details. Distribute to students a magazine article about music. Ask students to underline the main idea and circle the supporting details.

- At home, have each student meet with a family member to select a song—old or new—that the family likes. Have the student bring in a recording and play it (or sing it) for the class. Explain to the class why the family selected that song.

Use reading skills: Identify main idea and details. Remind students that they are always looking for the "big picture" of a story or article, trying to find the main idea and the supporting details. Often, the main idea, or topic, is stated in the opening sentence. Point students' attention to the paragraph on page 48 that begins, "The Fisk Jubilee Singers began singing all over the country." Then have them read the sentences that follow. Ask students to note that the rest of the paragraph gives details about where in the U.S. the singers sang and what they sang.

Use a graphic organizer. The diagram visually highlights the main idea and gives one exemplary supporting detail. It asks students to find two other details.

Using the graphic organizer will help the reader recognize other main ideas and supporting details in the article.

Write About It (PAGES 53–54)

Write sentences that tell what it was like to see the Fisk Jubilee Singers.   Have students read the directions at the top of page 53 and be sure they understand that they will write five sentences describing what it might have been like to see and hear the Fisk Jubilee Singers sing.

Prewriting   Have students imagine themselves in an audience hearing the Fisk Jubilee Singers perform. What was most interesting? How did the rest of the audience react? What surprised them? Tell them that these are the kinds of ideas that they will put in their graphic organizers.

Thinking Beyond Reading   Have students work with a partner or a small group to discuss the questions. The intent is for students to imagine what they will hear, see, and do as members of the Fisk audience. Encourage them to add details to their graphic organizers.

Write your sentences. Have students write independently. Be sure that students understand that each of the sentences they write must relate to what they see or hear on and off stage. While drafting, students should not be concerned with spelling or punctuation. Encourage them to write their sentences quickly and freely.

Revise and edit.   Remind students to use the Revising and Editing Checklist (Master 11) to guide them in revising their sentences. Have students review each other's sentences and give each other feedback, telling whether the sentences are logical, clear, and interesting. Have them check for capital letters, correct spelling, and punctuation.

When students have finished revising their writing, use the Writing Rubric (Master 10) to evaluate their sentences. Be sure you review the sentences with each student so he or she understands the strengths and weaknesses of this piece of writing. Have students date the writing and put it in their writing portfolios.

Building Fluency

Identify small sections from "The Fisk Jubilee Singers." Tell students that they will use choral reading to read these sections aloud. (See page 7 for a description of choral reading.) Give them time to read a passage silently 2–3 times to encourage the best oral reading. In order to set and maintain the pace, read along with the students. Identify words that cause the students to stumble. They will imitate the phrasing and intonation that you model. Remind students to use punctuation and typographic cues to add expression to their reading. Tell them that the goal is to read the passage as fluently as if they were just speaking.

The Rights of Citizens

Lesson Overview: (PAGE 55)

Theme

Have students read the lesson title on page 55 and tell them that the title introduces the lesson theme, Civics and Government. Discuss the theme by having students make personal connections, describing times when local, state, or federal government has been intertwined in their lives. Suggest that they think about legal concerns, licenses, voting, immigration, and many other daily concerns.

Learning Objectives

Be sure students understand the outcome of each of the learning goals.

- *Learn about how to become an American citizen.* Provide background, explaining that this article is nonfiction. It gives information that is true. It reports accurately about people and events and covers an issue that is critically important to many people. It is also often in today's news.
- *Learn to compare and contrast.*
- *Master the key vocabulary used in the article.*
- *Write sentences that tell what it might be like for an adult to become an American citizen.*

Preteach the vocabulary. (PAGE 55)

Read the key vocabulary words and their definitions to the students. Tell them that they will recognize all these words in the article.

- Distribute the Vocabulary Knowledge Rating Chart (Master 9) and have students individually rate each of the key vocabulary words.
- Preview particularly challenging words with students by listing each one on the board, modeling its use in a sentence, and having two or three students use the word in original sentences. Reframe student sentences that do not use the new words correctly.

You may wish to offer a mini-lesson on nouns as students read the respective parts of speech with the definitions of the vocabulary words. [See page 39 of this book for a mini-lesson on nouns. Use Master 1 or 2 to give students practice in recognizing nouns.]

Before You Read (PAGE 56)

Explain that active readers work to get the most from their reading. Good readers ask questions before, during, and after reading to better understand the meaning of the text. They make notes or write questions in the margins. They may also write if they agree or disagree with what they are reading. In other words, they get involved with what they are reading.

As students begin to write answers to the questions for each element on page 56, have them read the respective Think About Its in the side column.

Use what you know. Use the Think About It to elicit discussion about what students believe a person does to become an American citizen. In answering the questions, some students may discuss their own desires to become citizens or the process they went through to become citizens. Others will mention friends or relatives who have become naturalized citizens.

Ask yourself questions. Talk about why a person would want to become a U.S. citizen. Ask students to list their questions and write them on the board. Add questions to the list as students begin to read the article. You may want to keep track of the questions that are answered in the article to encourage students to consider this a reading strategy for much of their reading.

Reading the Article (PAGES 57–59)

Emphasize to students that reading to find out as much information as possible about becoming a citizen gives them a purpose for reading the passage. To keep them involved in the article, suggest that they make notes in the margin or in a small notebook as they find answers to their questions about the citizenship process.

Side-Column Vocabulary   Remind students that the vocabulary words and phrases in the side column have been selected as important to the theme and content of the story. These words may be useful in the context of becoming a citizen, but they are not necessarily part of everyday language.

Mid-Passage Questions   The answers to the questions are largely students' opinions, so there are not many right or wrong answers. Review students' written answers to assess whether they are getting meaning from the text. They might indicate in their answers that they are curious about what a citizenship ceremony is like or how many people become U.S. citizens every year.

After You Read (PAGES 60–61)

Build a robust vocabulary.   Ask students to check their answers in the answer keys in their books.

Think about your reading.   Ask students to check their answers in the answer keys in their books. Ask additional questions to enrich the discussion so that students will be better able to write about the experience of becoming an American citizen. Here are some possible questions:

- A good reader interacts with the text by imagining himself in the article. Imagine that you work at an information booth at an agency that gives out applications for people who want to become citizens. What are some of the questions people coming into the agency might ask?

- If you attended a party for a woman who had just become a citizen, what are some things you and the other guests might say to her?

Extend the reading   Here are some additional activities to expand the students' understanding.

- Ask students to interview a new U.S. citizen and write down why she wanted to become a citizen of this country. (Or ask a permanent resident why he wants to become a citizen.) Ask students to read the responses aloud.

- *For English Language Learners*   To explain the meaning of Walt Disney World to those not familiar with American culture, show pictures of children and families at the theme park. Talk about the kinds of rides and sights there, such as Magic Kingdom, Epcot, and others. Explain that many families go to Walt Disney World on vacation, eating in the restaurants, visiting the water parks, and seeing storybook characters. Make word cards with the words *restaurant*, *water park*, and *storybook characters* and ask students to match them to the correct photos.

- Give students additional practice in comparing and contrasting information. First, have students look at a picture of a soccer match, with fans of Team A (e.g. France) on one side of the stadium and fans of Team B (e.g. Brazil) on the other. Ask students to consider how the two sides are the same and different. Create a chart similar to the one on page 62 of the lesson, and label Col. 1 *Team A* and Col. 2 *Team B*. Ask students to list ways the spectators are different. Have the groups discuss and compare their answers. Then discuss ways the spectators are the same.

- At home, have each student try to find an application for a driver's license or a library card. Tell them to bring the applications to class. Explain what each is and how one fills it out.

Use reading skills: Compare and contrast.   Explain to students that authors have different approaches to comparing and contrasting information. Sometimes they describe one thing entirely, then go on to discuss the other entirely. Sometimes authors state an attribute and discuss how the first thing and the second thing fit that attribute, comparing and contrasting as they go. Explain that the author of "Becoming an American Citizen" followed the second approach. Ask students to find evidence of that.

Use a graphic organizer.   The chart in this lesson visually organizes what a citizen and a non-citizen can and cannot do. The graphic organizer helps students compare and contrast information.

Write About It (PAGES 63–64)

Write about what it might be like for an adult to become an American citizen. Have students read the directions on page 63 and be sure they understand that they will write five sentences describing what it might be like to become an American citizen as an adult.

Prewriting Have students think about what it would be like to become a citizen as a grown-up. Then ask them to discuss the process, the ceremony, and the new rights they will have. Tell them that these are the types of ideas that they will write in the ovals in their graphic organizer.

Thinking Beyond Reading Have students work with a partner or a small group to discuss the questions. The intent is for students to probe more deeply and to elaborate on the topic by imagining how they would feel as new citizens and why citizenship is important to them. Encourage them to add ideas to their graphic organizers as they talk.

Write your sentences. Have students write independently. Be sure that students understand that each of the sentences they write must relate to what life is like now that they are citizens. While drafting, students should not be concerned with spelling or punctuation. Encourage them to write their sentences quickly and freely.

Revise and edit. Remind students to use the Revising and Editing Checklist (Master 11) to guide them in revising their sentences. Have students review each other's sentences and give each other feedback, telling whether the sentences are logical, clear, and interesting. Have them check for capital letters, correct spelling, and punctuation.

When students have finished revising their writing, use the Writing Rubric (Master 10) to evaluate their sentences. Be sure you review the sentences with each student so he or she understands the strengths and weaknesses of this piece of writing. Have students date the writing and put it in their writing portfolios.

Building Fluency

Identify small sections from "Becoming an American Citizen." Tell students that they will use paired reading to read these sections aloud. Put students into groups of two. Give them time to read a passage silently 2–3 times to encourage their best oral reading. Partners take turns being the reader or listener. After the first reading, the listener does not provide feedback. After the second and third readings, the listener provides feedback to the reader. Remind students to pay attention to words that cause them to stumble and to read for the author's message. Their goal is to read the passage as fluently as if they were just speaking.

Learning to Swim

Lesson Overview: (PAGE 65)

Theme

Have students read the lesson title on page 65 and tell them that the title introduces the lesson theme, Sports and Recreation. Discuss the theme by having students make personal connections, describing sports they do and do not watch or play.

Learning Objectives

Be sure students understand the outcome of each of the learning goals.

- *Read a story about a man taking his first swimming lesson.* Point out to students that this story is fictional. Its characters are not real, but their problems are like those of people whom we all know. Many adults have fears they work to overcome.

- *Learn to predict outcomes.*

- *Master the key vocabulary used in the story.*

- *Write sentences that tell what it was like for you to do something for the first time.*

Preteach the vocabulary. (PAGE 65)

Read the key vocabulary words and their definitions to the students. Tell them that they will recognize all these words in the story.

- Distribute the Vocabulary Knowledge Rating Chart (Master 9) and have students individually rate each of the key vocabulary words.

- Preview particularly challenging words with students by listing each one on the board, modeling its use in a sentence, and having two or three students use the word in original sentences. Reframe student sentences that do not use the new words correctly.

You may wish to offer a mini-lesson on verbs as students read the respective parts of speech with the definitions of the vocabulary words. [See page 40 of this book for a mini-lesson on verbs. Use Master 3 or 4 to give students practice in recognizing verbs.]

Before You Read (PAGE 66)

Point out to students that good readers use a variety of strategies to be involved with what they read, and they will learn to select strategies that work best for them. One is to connect with the writing by considering what they already know or have experienced in their own lives related to the topic. Has anyone ever tried to do something for the first time as an adult? How did he or she feel?

Another useful strategy is to make predictions. If students read that a man is reluctant to take a swim lesson, they may predict that he could become afraid during the lesson or might even leave before the lesson is over. Then they can check to see if the prediction was correct.

As students begin to write answers to the questions for each element on page 66, have them read the respective Think About Its.

Use what you know.   Use the first Think About It to elicit discussion about an experience with someone they know who is very cautious or won't go into the water. In answering the questions, many students are likely to discuss how they feel about swimming, if they were ever scared, if they took swimming lessons, and so on.

Predict what will happen.   Have students read the first paragraph of "To Sink or Swim" and the first Think About It on page 66. What do students think will happen in the story? Do they think Ken will "sink" or "swim?" Encourage students to look for clues as to what Ken will do next.

Reading the Story (PAGES 67–69)

Emphasize to students that predicting what will happen next will keep them involved in the story. Suggest that they make notes in the margins or in a small notebook as they find clues. Then they can check to see if their predictions were correct.

Side-Column Vocabulary Remind students that the vocabulary words and phrases in the side column have been selected as important to the theme and content of the story. These words may be useful in the context of water and swimming lessons, but they are not necessarily part of everyday language.

Mid-Passage Questions The answers to the questions are largely students' opinions, so there are not many right or wrong answers. Review students' written answers to assess whether they are getting meaning from the text. They should indicate in their answers why Ken wants to learn to swim, and why he came out of the pool before the lesson was over.

After You Read (PAGES 70–71)

Build a robust vocabulary. Ask students to check their answers in the answer keys in their books.

Think about your reading. Ask students to check their answers in the answer keys in their books. Ask additional questions to enrich the discussion so that students will be better able to write about what it was like for them to do something for the first time. Here are some possible questions:

- Would you describe Ken as wise or foolish to try to learn to swim as an adult? What makes you say that?

- Imagine that Ken goes home and does not complete his first swimming lesson. How do you think he feels? What do you think he'll do the following day? Why is it hard for Ken to learn to swim so late in life? Explain your answers.

   Extend the reading. Here are some additional activities to expand the students' understanding.

   - Imagine that Ken is talking to his 34-year-old sister Marie. Once he has learned to swim, what are two things he might say to her to convince her to take swimming lessons, too? Have students dramatize Ken talking to Marie.

- *For English Language Learners* Explain that the word *headed* in "He headed across the locker room" in the last paragraph of the story means to set off or go in a certain direction. Although the word *head* appears in *headed*, one's *head* has nothing to do with the term. Ask students to tell where they are *headed* after this class. Have students add this phrase to their personal dictionaries.

- Point out to students that the predictions they make as they read a fiction story should be based on the personalities of the characters whom they get to know better as they read more of the story. Ask students to re-examine the story to see when they thought Ken would learn to swim and when they thought he would give up. Have them make a list of Ken's characteristics that supported their predictions. Did their ideas change as they read the story?

- At home, have each student find a magazine or newspaper photo that prompts a discussion of something they would like to learn to do, such as fix a flat tire or use a new food processor. Ask them to bring the photos to class and discuss.

Use reading skills: Predict outcomes. Experienced readers know that an important skill when reading fiction is to predict what will happen before they read it. That is, they keep identifying clues in the story, then they think of likely things that a character will do next. Their predictions are often based on what they have experienced and on people whom they know. Many students will say that Ken is so cautious about the water that he will never succeed as a swimmer. Others will know from experience how children can motivate their parents to succeed at things. Students will have different opinions of how much perseverance Ken has.

Use a graphic organizer. The prediction chart in this lesson helps students read the clues and keep track of their predictions as they read the story. A graphic organizer can help students focus on smaller elements in the story and remember that different events bring out different aspects of the character.

Write About It (PAGES 73–74)

Write sentences about a time when you did something for the first time. Have students read the directions on page 73 and be sure they understand that they will write five sentences telling what it was like to do something for the first time.

Prewriting Have students think about what it was like to do something for the first time. Then ask them to discuss what they did, and the order in which the events took place. Tell them that these are the types of ideas that they will write in their graphic organizers.

Thinking Beyond Reading Have students work with a partner or a small group to discuss the questions. The intent is for students to probe more deeply and to elaborate on the topic by recalling what they did for the first time, when it happened, what they did first, next, and last. Encourage them to add ideas to their charts.

Write your sentences. Have students write independently. Be sure that students understand that all the sentences must relate to what it was like to learn a new skill or handle a new task. While drafting, students should not be concerned with spelling or punctuation. Encourage them to write their sentences quickly and freely.

Revise and edit. Remind students to use the Revising and Editing Checklist (Master 11) to guide them in revising their sentences. Have students review each other's writing and give each other feedback, telling whether the sentences are logical, clear, and interesting. Have them check for capital letters, correct spelling, and punctuation.

When students have finished revising their writing, use the Writing Rubric (Master 10) to evaluate their sentences. Be sure you review the sentences with each student so he or she understands the strengths and weaknesses of this piece of writing. Have students date the writing and put it in their writing portfolios.

Building Fluency

Identify small sections from "To Sink or Swim." Tell students that they will use echo reading to read these sections aloud. (See page 7 for a description of echo reading.) Put students into groups of two. Give them time to read a passage silently 2–3 times to encourage their best oral reading. Remind them to pay attention to words that cause them to stumble. They will imitate your phrasing and intonation for each sentence. Remind students to use punctuation and typographic cues to add expression to their reading. Tell them that the goal is to read the passage as fluently as if they were just speaking.

Transportation Troubles

Lesson Overview: (PAGE 75)

Theme

Have students read the lesson title on page 75 and tell them that the title introduces the lesson theme, Transportation. Discuss the theme by having students make personal connections, describing transportation they take to work or for recreation.

Learning Objectives

Be sure students understand the outcome of each of the learning goals.

- *Read a story about a man who must find a way to get to work when he can't take the bus.* Point out to students that this story is fictional. Its characters are not real, but their problems are like those of people whom we all know. Anyone could find himself in a situation similar to Lou's, without a car, bus, or train available to get to work the next day.

- *Learn to make inferences.*

- *Master the key vocabulary used in the story.*

- *Write sentences that tell about how you would get to work if your usual means of transportation were not available.*

Preteach the vocabulary. (PAGE 75)

Read the key vocabulary words and their definitions to the students. Tell them that they will recognize all these words in the story.

- Distribute the Vocabulary Knowledge Rating Chart (Master 9) and have students individually rate each of the key vocabulary words.

- Preview particularly challenging words with students by listing each one on the board, modeling its use in a sentence, and having two or three students use the word in original sentences. Reframe student sentences that do not use the new words correctly.

You may wish to offer a mini-lesson on adverbs as students read the respective parts of speech with the definitions of the vocabulary words. [See page 42 of this book for a mini-lesson on adverbs. Use Master 7 or 8 to give students practice in recognizing adverbs.]

Before You Read (PAGE 76)

Explain that active readers get involved in the reading. They constantly make connections between their own prior knowledge and the story they are reading. They look for story clues to understand what is happening to the characters. In other words, the reader notices what has occurred and how the events affect each character. Lou has a problem regarding his transportation to work during a labor strike, and his girlfriend is involved in the problem as well. The problem, therefore, affects their relationship. Many students will have a personal connection to the transportation problem or in living with someone who is struggling with a problem. Suggest to students that they underline sentences in the story that remind them of events in their lives.

As students begin to write answers to the questions for each element on page 76, have them read the respective Think About Its.

Set a purpose for reading. Have students read the title "How Many Ways to Get to Work?" and the first Think About It. Ask what they picture in their minds when they think of transportation problems. Ask students why they want to read this story—will they learn anything from it? Do they think the situation will apply to their own lives?

Use what you know. Use the second Think About It to elicit discussion about instances when students were late to work. In answering the questions, many students are likely to discuss a time when buses or subways were late or when their cars broke down, and they were delayed getting to work. Have them recall the emotions of that day and respond personally to the problem in the story.

Reading the Story (PAGES 77–79)

Emphasize that reading to learn about Lou's problem and how he solves it gives students a purpose for reading the passage. Highlighting sentences that describe the transportation problem will keep them involved in the story.

Side-Column Vocabulary Remind students that the vocabulary words and phrases in the side column have been selected as important to the theme and content of the story. These words may be useful in the context of transportation, but they are not necessarily part of everyday language.

Mid-Passage Questions The answers to some questions are largely students' opinions, so there are not many right or wrong answers. Review students' written answers to assess whether they are getting meaning from the text. They should indicate in their answers how they would feel if the bus they normally took to work wasn't running.

After You Read (PAGES 80–81)

Build a robust vocabulary. Ask students to check their answers in the answer keys in their books.

Think about your reading. Ask students to check their answers in the answer keys in their books. Ask additional questions to enrich the discussion so that students will be better able to write about how they would get to work if their usual transportation were unavailable. Here are some possible questions:

- Would you describe Lou as brave or foolish to take his bike to work during the strike? Why?

- Imagine that a fellow worker asks Lou to pick him up and give him a ride to work on the back of Lou's bike. What do you think Lou would say or do? Explain.

Extend the reading. Here are some additional activities to expand the students' understanding.

- Make a list of two other ways Lou could have gotten to work on the first day of the strike.

Explain why they would or wouldn't be better than a bike.

- *For English Language Learners* Explain that the word *bet* as in "And the strike will be over soon, I *bet*" means that Rosa feels sure the strike will be resolved soon. In other contexts, *bet* can mean to gamble, as when people place *bets* on horse races. Have students add this phrase to their personal dictionaries.

- Give students additional practice in making inferences. Ask them to think how a change in Rosa's job status would affect the situation. Draw on the board a chart like the one on page 82. Divide students into pairs. Have students imagine that Rosa has been laid off from her job. Have Student A write that in the first column. Have the same student write in the second column what he or she knows about how layoffs affect people. Have Student B write in the third column his inference regarding Rosa's and Lou's relationship. For example, Rosa and Lou may start arguing about how they will have enough money for food and rent. Have the pairs discuss and compare their charts.

- At home, have each student find a magazine or newspaper photo of a way Lou may *wish* he could get to work every day. Ask them to bring the photos to class and discuss.

Use reading skills: Make inferences. Experienced readers know that making inferences is important in understanding fiction. The reader reads "between the lines" by identifying clues in the story from what a character says or does, or from what the author says about the character. Then the reader considers what she knows about that character and makes an inference about what the character might do next. Do students think that Rosa was supportive to Lou when he was upset about getting to work? From this, what do they infer about the couple's relationship? Do students infer that Rosa will be pleased by Lou riding his bike to work? Why do they think that?

Use a graphic organizer. The inference chart helps students pay attention to the story clues, helps them consider what they know about the characters and their problems, and then helps them make inferences about the characters' behaviors. A graphic organizer like this one helps the reader understand how the story plot unfolds.

Write About It (PAGES 83–84)

Write sentences about how you would get to work if your usual means of transportation were not available. Have students read the directions on page 83 and be sure they understand that they will write five sentences telling what they would do if they had to find another way to get to work.

Prewriting Have students think about a time they had trouble getting to work. Then ask them to discuss what they did and how they solved the problem. Tell them that these are the types of ideas they will write in their graphic organizers.

Thinking Beyond Reading Have students work with a partner or a small group to discuss the questions. The intent is for students to probe more deeply into the transportation problem and consider a range of ideas about what people do to get to work when their regular means of travel is unavailable. Encourage them to add ideas to their graphic organizers.

Write Sentences Have students write independently. Be sure that students understand that all the sentences must relate to things they would do to get to work if the regular way was unavailable. While drafting, students should not be concerned with spelling or punctuation. Encourage them to write their sentences quickly and freely.

Revise and edit. Remind students to use the Revising and Editing Checklist (Master 11) to guide them in revising their sentences. Have students review each other's writing and give each other feedback, telling whether the sentences are logical, clear, and interesting. Have them check for capital letters, correct spelling, and punctuation.

When students have finished revising their writing, use the Writing Rubric (Master 10) to evaluate their sentences. Be sure you review the sentences with each student so he or she understands the strengths and weaknesses of this piece of writing. Have students date the writing and put it in their writing portfolios.

Building Fluency

Identify small sections from "How Many Ways to Get to Work?" Tell students that they will use paired reading to read these sections aloud. Put students into groups of two. Give them time to read a passage silently 2–3 times to encourage their best oral reading. Partners take turns being the reader or listener. After the first reading, the listener does not provide feedback. After the second and third readings, the listener provides feedback to the reader. Remind students to pay attention to words that cause them to stumble and to read for the author's message. Their goal is to read the passage as fluently as if they were just speaking.

Food for Thought

Lesson Overview: (PAGE 85)

Theme

Have students read the lesson title on page 85 and tell them that the title introduces the lesson theme, Food. Discuss the theme by having students make personal connections, describing favorite foods and foods they like to prepare.

Learning Objectives

Be sure students understand the outcome of each of the learning goals.

- *Read a story about a woman who uses her grandmother's cookie recipe.* Point out to students that this story is fiction. The characters are not real, but their activities, conversations, and problems are similar to those of people we all know.
- *Learn to identify time order.*
- *Master the key vocabulary used in the article.*
- *Write sentences that tell about a time when you made something good to eat.*

Preteach the vocabulary. (PAGE 85)

Read the key vocabulary words and their definitions to the students. Tell them that they will recognize all these words in the story.

- Distribute the Vocabulary Knowledge Rating Chart (Master 9) and have students individually rate each of the key vocabulary words.
- Preview particularly challenging words with students by listing each one on the board, modeling its use in a sentence, and having two or three students use the word in original sentences. Reframe student sentences that do not use the new words correctly.

You may wish to offer a mini-lesson on nouns as students read the respective parts of speech with the definitions of the vocabulary words. [See page 39 of this book for a mini-lesson on nouns. Use Master 1 or 2 to give students practice in recognizing nouns.]

Before You Read (PAGE 86)

Explain that good readers select strategies that suit their purpose. One effective strategy might be for students to make connections between their own experiences and the story they are reading. Do students have a favorite family recipe? Do they understand why Tina wants to make biscotti that are as good as her grandmother's? Once students know that the story is about Tina's desire to make a cookie just as good as her grandmother's, they may predict her problems and how she will overcome them. Then they will read on to see if their predictions are correct.

As students begin to write answers to the questions for each element on page 86, have them read the respective Think About Its.

Use what you know. Use the first Think About It to elicit discussion about foods students like to eat or prepare. In answering the questions, many students are likely to discuss recipes they have tried. Encourage them to share which recipes were successes and which were not. Do students know why the failed recipes were not successful? Did they ever make those recipes again?

Make predictions. Have students read the first paragraph of "The Right Recipe" and the second Think About It. As they read the rest of the story, have students predict what will happen when Tina makes her grandmother's recipe for biscotti. Ask students to predict whether they think this story will have a happy ending. Ask them to tell why.

Reading the Story (PAGES 87–89)

Emphasize to students that reading to learn about Tina's problem with a recipe gives them a purpose for reading the story. Suggest that they will stay more involved in the story if they use a highlighter to mark clues to the solution to Tina's problem. They may discover that some of the clues do not lead directly to the solution.

Side-Column Vocabulary   Remind students that the vocabulary words and phrases in the side column have been selected as important to the theme and content of the story. These words may be useful in the context of baking cookies, but they are not necessarily part of everyday language.

Mid-Passage Questions   Some answers to the questions are largely students' opinions, so there are not many right or wrong answers. Review students' written answers to assess whether they are getting meaning from the text. They should indicate in their answers what they think Tina will do next.

After You Read (PAGES 90–91)

Build a robust vocabulary.   Ask students to check their answers in the answer keys in their books.

Think about your reading.   Ask students to check their answers in the answer keys in their books. Ask additional questions to enrich the discussion so that students will be better able to write about a time when they made something good to eat. Here are some possible questions:

- Would the story be different if Tina had had a grater? Does the right equipment in the kitchen make a significant difference?

- Imagine that a friend asks you for a recipe that has been a secret in your family for years. Would you share your recipe? Explain your answer.

Extend the reading.   Here are some additional activities to expand the students' understanding.

- Imagine that Tina is making a scrapbook of memories of her grandmother. What kinds of pictures and photos would go in the scrapbook? Why would you choose those photos?

- *For English Language Learners*   Explain that the phrase *that doesn't matter* on page 88 means "It's not important." Have students think of instances in which they might say something, then follow it with "It doesn't matter." Have

students add this phrase to their personal dictionaries.

- Give students additional practice in identifying time order. Ask them to think about the steps Tina took when she asked her husband, son, and brother to taste her biscotti. Draw on the board a chart like the one on page 92. Have students think of the steps in the order that Tina followed. Have students number the lines 1–5. Then have students write in the five things Tina did in the process, using the language of time order: *first, then, next, finally,* and so on. Have students compare their charts.

- At home, have each student find a recipe for a favorite family dish. Tell them to bring the recipe to class and discuss. If possible, have students make the dish at home and bring samples to class.

Use reading skills: Identify time order.   Experienced readers know that keeping track of the sequence of events in a story is important to comprehending fiction. It is an important part of the text structure, the way that the author organizes the story. Point out to students that they should make sense of the time order even if the author writes the events out of sequence. Help students note that writers often use signal words such as *first, next, then,* and *last* to present the sequence of events in the story. By focusing on time order, students can understand how one event leads to another.

Use a graphic organizer.   The time-order chart helps students focus on events in the proper sequence. Use a graphic organizer. helps the reader understand how events in the story are organized.

Write About It (PAGES 93–94)

Write about a time that you made something that tasted really good.   Have students read the directions on the top of page 93 and be sure they understand that they will write five sentences telling what they prepared and how it tasted.

Prewriting   Have students think about a time when they prepared an excellent dish or meal. Tell them that they will write about how they did it in their graphic organizers.

Thinking Beyond Reading Have students work with a partner or a small group to discuss the questions. The intent is for students to address issues that did not arise when they were first thinking about the foods they prepared and the steps they took in making it.

Write your sentences. Have students write their sentences independently. Be sure that students understand that all the sentences must relate to what they prepared and how it tasted. Remind students to use the steps chart to organize the five steps. While drafting, students should not be concerned with spelling or punctuation. Encourage them to write their sentences quickly and freely.

Revise and edit. Remind students to use the Revising and Editing Checklist (Master 11) to guide them in revising their sentences. Have students review each other's sentences and give each other feedback, telling whether the sentences are logical, clear, and interesting. Have them check for capital letters, correct spelling, and punctuation.

When students have finished revising their writing, use the Writing Rubric (Master 10) to evaluate their sentences. Be sure you review the sentences with each student so he or she understands the strengths and weaknesses of this piece of writing. Have students date the writing and put it in their writing portfolios.

Building Fluency

Identify small sections from "The Right Recipe." Tell students that they will use paired reading to read these sections aloud. Put students into groups of two. Give them time to read a passage silently 2–3 times to encourage their best oral reading. Partners take turns being the reader or listener. After the first reading, the listener does not provide feedback. After the second and third readings, the listener provides feedback to the reader. Remind students to pay attention to words that cause them to stumble and to read for the author's message. Their goal is to read the passage as fluently as if they were just speaking.

Trading Clothes, Saving Money

Lesson Overview: (PAGE 95)

Theme

Have students read the lesson title on page 95 and tell them that the title introduces the lesson theme, Consumerism and Money. Discuss the theme by having students make personal connections, describing how they budget, spend, and save money.

Learning Objectives

Be sure students understand the outcome of each of the learning goals.

- *Learn about a way to trade old clothes for new ones.* Provide background, explaining that this article is nonfiction. The trend that it describes, clothing swaps, is catching on around the United States. The article gives factual information and reports accurately about people and events that have actually taken place.

- *Learn to synthesize information.*

- *Master the key vocabulary used in the article.*

- *Write sentences that tell what it might be like to go to a clothing swap.*

Preteach the vocabulary. (PAGE 95)

Read the key vocabulary words and their definitions to the students. Tell them that they will recognize all these words in the article.

- Distribute the Vocabulary Knowledge Rating Chart (Master 9) and have students individually rate each of the key vocabulary words.

- Preview particularly challenging words with students by listing each one on the board, modeling its use in a sentence, and having two or three students use the word in original sentences. Reframe student sentences that do not use the new words correctly.

You may wish to offer a mini-lesson on adjectives as students read the respective parts of speech with the definitions of the vocabulary words. [See page 41 of this book for a mini-lesson on adjectives. Use Master 5 or 6 to give students practice in recognizing adjectives.]

Before You Read (PAGE 96)

Explain that active readers get more out of their reading. As they read, they constantly make connections between their own prior experiences and the passage they are reading. Ask students if they have ever tried to save money when buying their own or their children's clothing. Remind them to ask what they want to get from their reading. Might the article suggest some ways to acquire new clothing without spending more money? Might they get some ideas they can apply in their own lives? Suggest they put a star next to ideas they read that they think could be useful to them.

As students begin to write answers to the questions for each element on page 96, have them read the respective Think About Its.

Use what you know. Use the first Think About It to elicit discussion about purchasing and wearing clothing. In answering the questions, many students are likely to recall times when they were not satisfied with their purchases or when they bought an article of clothing and regretted it because they wore it only once.

Set a purpose for reading. Have students read the title "Old Clothes for New" and discuss what the title means. Have they heard of clothing swaps? What would they like to know about them? Suggest that they will read to find out what they are, who goes to them, where they are held, and whether people are satisfied with their purchases.

Reading the Article (PAGES 97–99)

Emphasize to students that reading to learn how an organized clothing swap works gives them a purpose for reading the passage. Highlighting important facts will keep them involved in the article and will help them recall what they have learned.

Side-Column Vocabulary Remind students that the vocabulary words and phrases in the side column have been selected as important to the theme and content of the story. These words may be useful in the context of shopping and money, but they are not necessarily part of everyday language.

Mid-Passage Questions Some answers to the questions are largely students' opinions, so there are not many right or wrong answers. Review students' written answers to assess whether they are getting meaning from the text. They should indicate in their answers that some people who run clothing swaps charge money so they can make a profit. Students should also mention that clothing swaps used to be held in people's homes, but have now become bigger events and are often held in public places.

After You Read (PAGES 100–101)

Build a robust vocabulary. Ask students to check their answers in the answer keys in their books.

Think about your reading. Ask students to check their answers in the answer keys in their books. Ask additional questions to enrich the discussion so that students will be better able to write about what it's like to go to a clothing swap. Here are some possible questions:

- A good reader makes comparisons. Ask students to consider in what ways shopping in a department store and going to a clothing swap are the same and different.

- Ask students to visualize what would happen if two people at a clothing swap want the same item. Suggest they think about the conversation that might take place between the two people. How persuasive could each of the two people be?

Extend the Reading Here are some additional activities to expand the students' understanding.

- Ask students to imagine that they run a clothing swap in their neighborhood. They are about to post a list of rules or guidelines for the swap. What would the guidelines say?

- *For English Language Learners* Explain that to "flip a coin" is the practice of flipping a coin in the air to resolve a dispute between two people. Point out that one person calls *heads* and the other person calls *tails*. Explain that the outcome is due to luck. Have students flip a coin ten times and see which student wins the majority of rounds. Have students add this phrase to their personal dictionaries.

- At home, have students look through their closets and make lists of the clothing items they would bring to a clothing swap. In class, have students explain the reason why they would be willing to trade each of those items. They can also describe the items they would hope to find at a clothing swap.

Use reading skills: Synthesize information. Help students understand that their job as readers is to synthesize or combine pieces of information. As they identify key ideas in the text or become aware of new ideas or additional facts, they combine that new information with what they already know.

Use a graphic organizer. The chart in this lesson helps students recognize what they already know about buying clothing, what they learned in the article, and what new idea they come to by putting these together. Using this type of graphic organizer helps readers synthesize information that they can apply to their own lives.

Write About It (PAGES 103–104)

Write about going to a clothing swap. Have students read the directions on the top of page 103. Be sure they understand that they will write five sentences describing what it might be like to go to a clothing swap.

Prewriting Have students consider what it might be like to attend a clothing swap. Ask them to discuss who would be there, when it would be held, and what kinds of clothing would be available. Tell them that these are the types of ideas that they will write in the ovals in their graphic organizers.

Thinking Beyond Reading Have students work with a partner or a small group to discuss the questions. The intent is for students to probe more deeply and to elaborate on the topic by imagining themselves bringing clothing, evaluating others' clothing, and making exchanges at a clothing swap. Encourage them to add ideas to their webs.

Write your sentences. Have students write independently. Be sure that students understand that all the sentences must relate to what it's like to be at a clothing swap. Remind students to use the ideas in their webs to organize the different elements of their descriptions. While drafting, students should not be concerned with spelling or punctuation. Encourage them to write their sentences quickly and freely.

Revise and edit. Remind students to use the Revising and Editing Checklist (Master 11) to guide them in revising their sentences. Have students review each other's sentences and give each other feedback, telling whether the sentences are logical, clear, and interesting. Have them check for capital letters, correct spelling, and punctuation.

When students have finished revising their writing, use the Writing Rubric (Master 10) to evaluate their sentences. Be sure you review the sentences with each student so he or she understands the strengths and weaknesses of this piece of writing. Have students date the writing and put it in their writing portfolios.

Building Fluency

Identify small sections from "Old Clothes for New." Tell students that they will use paired reading to read these sections aloud. Put students into groups of two. Give them time to read a passage silently 2–3 times to encourage their best oral reading. Partners take turns being the reader or listener. After the first reading, the listener does not provide feedback. After the second and third readings, the listener provides feedback to the reader. Remind students to pay attention to words that cause them to stumble and to read for the author's message. Their goal is to read the passage as fluently as if they were just speaking.

Grammar Mini-Lessons

LESSON 1: NOUNS

Learning Objectives

To define the term *noun*

To identify nouns

To generate nouns

Activate Prior Knowledge

Help students recall or find out what they already know about *nouns*. Have the class play a movie guessing game. Ask a volunteer to begin by giving one-word clues that name the people, places, and things in a recent movie they saw. Write on the board the nouns they use. (Examples: *cops, robbers, cars, wizard, Hogwarts*) Encourage the student to continue to give clues until someone guesses the name of the movie.

Tell students that the clues they used are the names of the people (characters), places (locations), and things (props) used in the movie and that such words are called **nouns.**

Instruction

Tell the class that **nouns are the names of people, places, and things.** Write this definition on the board. Then have students help you create a noun chart.

Examples of Nouns		
People	**Places**	**Things**

Tell students that you see things everywhere around you every day. The names of these things are nouns. Ask students to list the people they see every day *(teacher, messenger, waiter)*, then the places they are in every day *(classroom, building, café)*, and finally, the names of things they use every day *(pen, jacket, desk)*. Write the common nouns they offer in the proper columns of the chart. When the chart is filled in, ask: What are these words? *(nouns)* What do they name? *(people, places, things)*

If students suggest proper nouns, include them. Point out to students that a proper noun can be a person's name, the name of a city or a state, a street name, the name of a month, or a holiday. Also point out that proper nouns are written with a capital letter at the beginning of each word.

Noun Practice

For more student practice with nouns, distribute Master 1 or 2 in this Teacher's Guide.

LESSON 2: VERBS

Learning Objectives
To define the term *verb*

To identify verbs

To generate verbs

Activate Prior Knowledge
Help students recall or find out what they already know about *verbs*. Have volunteers tell how to get to their classroom from the front door. Get them started by saying, "Go to the front door," and write the word *Go* on the board. In order to generate a variety of verbs, tell students that once a word is written on the board, it cannot be used again.

As students give directions, write the verbs they use on the board. (Examples: *Take a left. Walk down the hall. Stop at the exit sign. Make a right. Climb the steps. Turn right again.*) Encourage them to use silly words if they cannot think of realistic ones. (Examples: *Jump through the door. Skip across the hall.*)

When students are done, write the word *verbs* above the list. Tell students that all of these words are **verbs.**

Instruction
Tell the class that **words that show action are called verbs.** Write the following on the board: *Squirrels scurry up a tree. Seagulls swoop from the sky.* With students, identify the subject of each sentence. *(squirrels, seagulls)* Then, to help them identify the verb, ask: *What does the (subject) do? What is the action? (scurry, swoop)* Point out that the words they identify are verbs. Ask: What does a verb show? *(action)*

Encourage students to generate verbs of their own. Ask them to work in pairs to create oral sentences telling what other actions are performed by the same subjects. (Examples: *Squirrels eat acorns/eat; Seagulls fly over garbage dumps/fly*) Have them identify the verbs orally and write their verbs on the board. Ask: What are words that show action? *(verbs)*

Encourage students to compose additional oral sentences, each using a verb that tells about their own actions. Model sentences for them by writing on the board: *Today I _____. Yesterday I _____. Tomorrow I _____.* (Example: *study, studied, will study*) Point out that verbs also show time.

Verb Practice
For more student practice with verbs, distribute Master 3 or 4 in this Teacher's Guide.

LESSON 3: ADJECTIVES

Learning Objectives

To define the term *adjective*

To identify adjectives

To generate adjectives

Activate Prior Knowledge

Help students recall or discover what they already know about *adjectives*. Invite the class to describe some animals. For example, ask: *What characteristics make an elephant different from other animals?* Write on the board their responses, phrases consisting of a noun plus adjectives. (Examples: *big ears, tiny tail, huge body, two tusks, long nose/ long trunk*) Then underline the adjectives. Tell the class that these words describe nouns. They are called **adjectives.**

Instruction

Tell the class that **adjectives are words that describe nouns.** They tell how a noun looks, tastes, smells, feels, or sounds. Draw the following chart on the board. Ask the class to help you complete it. Write an example of your own to help them get started.

Nouns	Adjectives	
spider	brown scary	large hairy
.		

Elicit nouns from the class and write two or three in the first column. You may wish to have them name animals, insects, or items that they see every day. (Examples: *pigeon, squirrel, chipmunk, ladybug, mosquito, pencil, book*) Then have volunteers take turns writing a word in the adjective column to describe each noun. Finally, have volunteers use both a noun and an adjective from the chart in an oral sentence.

You may wish to point out to students that a noun may be described with more than one adjective. Read aloud a noun and two or more adjectives from the chart in your own sentence. *(Example: A large, scary spider was hiding in my boot.)* Have volunteers do the same.

Have students work in pairs to create their own charts. Suggest including nouns that hold some meaning to them. (Examples: *children, friends, easel, guitar, carpentry, machinery*) Invite volunteers to share their nouns and adjectives in oral sentences.

Adjective Practice

For more student practice with adjectives, distribute Master 5 or 6 in this Teacher's Guide.

LESSON 4: ADVERBS

Learning Objectives

To define the term *adverb*

To identify adverbs

To generate adverbs

Activate Prior Knowledge

Help students recall or find out what they already know about adverbs. Ask a volunteer to describe his or her routines in the morning. Listen carefully and then summarize the description by writing on the board a verb with an adverb. (Examples: *wakes early, washes sleepily, dresses quickly, drinks fast*) Write a second verb phrase that includes an adverb. Underline each verb, reminding students *These are verbs.* Then draw a circle around each of the adverbs, telling the class that these words are **adverbs.** They describe the action.

Instruction

Tell the class that **adverbs are words that describe verbs.** They describe the action of the verb in more detail. Draw a chart like the one shown below on the board. Elicit common verbs from the class and list them in the left column. (Examples: *run, walk, write, talk*)

Verbs	Adverbs

Then elicit from volunteers one word that describes each of the verbs. You may wish to give an example of your own to get them started. (Examples: *run—fast; read—carefully, slowly; write—neatly, sloppily; talk—softly, loudly*) As they respond, write their words in the right column. Add the header "Adverbs" to the right column. Ask students: *What kind of words did you use to describe the action of the verbs? (adverbs)*

Point out that many adverbs answer one of the following questions: how, when, or where. Write on the board two sentences, one with no adverbs and one with an adverb. (Examples: *The baby cried.* and *The baby cried loudly.*) Point to the subject and verb of the first sentence, ask how the baby cried, and underline the adverb in the second sentence. Repeat the exercise with other sentences, this time asking the class to add a word that answers the question *when.* Repeat for the question *where.* (Examples: *The officer directed traffic; The officer directed traffic today. The officer directed traffic here.*)

Adverb Practice

For more student practice with adverbs, distribute Master 7 or 8 in this Teacher's Guide.

Master 1: Nouns 1

Student's Name _____

A noun is the name of a person, place, or thing.

People	woman	Mildred Taylor
Places	state	Ohio
Things	book	*The Land*

Finding Nouns: Underline the nouns. HINT: There are two nouns in each sentence.

1. Her home is in Alabama.

2. Coretta studies the violin.

3. The couple married in church.

4. Martin was her husband.

5. They stayed in India for a month.

6. People remember him as a hero.

7. His birthday is now a holiday.

Writing Nouns: One of the words in each pair is a noun. Write the nouns.

8. paper, pointed _____

9. silky, soup _____

10. honey, heavy _____

11. healthy, hair _____

12. song, sour _____

13. angle, angry _____

14. curvy, cube _____

15. boxes, big _____

Using Nouns: Write a noun to complete each sentence.

16. We walked to the _____.

17. The _____ welcomed us.

18. We looked at the _____.

19. The _____ was on sale.

20. We waited for the _____.

Master 2: Nouns 2

Student's Name _____

> **A noun is the name of a person, place, or thing.**

Examples of nouns are listed in the chart below.

People	mechanic	waiter	nurse
Places	garage	tavern	clinic
Things	car	food	bandage

Finding Nouns: Underline the nouns. HINT: There are two in each sentence.

1. The friends jog in the park.

2. They see a chipmunk on the path.

3. They hear children in the playground.

4. The cars are parked on the street.

5. Mothers watch the babies play.

6. Busy people hurry to the office.

7. The family walks to the tall fountain.

Writing Nouns: Read the list of nouns. Write one to complete each sentence.

| rooftops | pigeons | pizza | jungle | home | Argentina |

8. There are wild _____ in Brooklyn.

9. They often perch on _____.

10. They eat seeds and sometimes eat _____.

11. They came from the country of _____.

12. Some say the birds escaped from the _____.

13. Now they call the U.S. their _____.

Using Nouns: Write a noun to complete each sentence.

14. I shovel the _____.

15. I sweep the _____.

16. I dust the _____.

17. I scrub the _____.

18. I wash the _____.

Master 3: Verbs 1

Student's Name _____

A verb is a word that shows action.

The underlined words are verbs. They show action.

<u>Take</u> a deep breath.   <u>Close</u> your eyes.
<u>Flap</u> your arms.   <u>Dive</u> in the water.

Finding Verbs: Circle the verb in each sentence.

1. They race on their bicycles.

2. The events begin in the spring.

3. The riders travel over steep hills.

4. He pedals very fast.

5. They steer around rocks and holes.

6. She hops the bike in tight circles.

7. They respect his special style.

Writing Verbs: Underline the verbs. Then write them on the line. HINT: One sentence has two verbs.

8. The bed sags in the middle. _____

9. She jumps on it anyway. _____

10. She leaps into the air. _____

11. She stretches her arms over her head. _____

12. She kicks her feet up high. _____

13. She reaches for the ceiling. _____

14. The bed sways and creaks. _____

15. We hear her laughter all through the house. _____

Using Verbs: Show the action. Write a verb to complete each sentence.

Example: ___*Climb*___ the tree.

16. _____ the boat.

17. _____ on the track.

18. _____ the fly ball.

19. _____ on the swings.

20. _____ the burger.

21. _____ on the grass.

Master 4: Verbs 2

Student's Name _____

> **A verb is a word that shows action.**

Read the underlined verbs. They show action.

Present	Past	Future
He <u>plays</u>.	He <u>played</u>.	He <u>will play</u>.
He <u>bikes</u>.	He <u>biked</u>.	He <u>will bike</u>.
He <u>skates</u>.	He <u>skated</u>.	He <u>will skate</u>.

Finding Verbs: The verb in each sentence is underlined. Circle the time it shows.

1. The man <u>climbed</u> the mountain.   present   past

2. A girl <u>stumbled</u> through the woods.   past   future

3. He <u>finds</u> the lost youngster.   present   past

4. The girl <u>walked</u> away from camp.   past   future

5. She <u>follows</u> the trail.   past   present

6. Her father <u>will wait</u> for her.   future   present

Writing Verbs: Underline the verb in each sentence. Then write the verb on the line.

7. Tiger swings with power and grace. _____

8. He will win more games than anyone else. _____

9. He earned a great many awards. _____

10. Woods breaks records all the time. _____

11. He defended his title more than once. _____

12. He usually completes the season on top. _____

Using Verbs: Underline the verbs. Then write a verb that shows a different time.

Example: The doors <u>opened</u>. ____*will open*_____

13. Trains raced through the tunnel. _____

14. Loud noises filled the air. _____

15. Wheels pounded the tracks. _____

16. They rumbled to a stop. _____

17. People rushed out the doors. _____

Master 5: Adjectives 1

Student's Name _____

> **An adjective is a word that describes a noun.**

The adjectives are underlined. They describe the nouns.

<u>sad</u> smile	<u>playful</u> pup	<u>shiny</u> pebbles
<u>soft</u> sounds	<u>sweet</u> apple	<u>brown</u> bears
<u>hot</u> cocoa	<u>two</u> students	<u>huge</u> acorns

Finding Adjectives: Read each sentence. Then underline the adjective that BEST describes the noun.

1. We hop into the big (wet, dry) puddle.

2. Then we climb the (funny, tall) tree.

3. She dives into the (cool, fiery) lake.

4. Let's play a (soft, good) game of volleyball.

5. She slides and rips her (blue, dainty) jeans.

6. The (friendly, sad) pair laugh out loud.

7. They walk back to their (cozy, short) home.

Writing Adjectives: Write the adjective that describes the underlined noun.

8. His first <u>job</u> is handing out newspapers. _____

9. Then he waits tables at the new <u>diner</u>. _____

10. His bright <u>mind</u> is filled with questions. _____

11. He does not want to build tall <u>towers</u>. _____

12. Going to distant <u>stars</u> is not in his plan. _____

13. The proud <u>man</u> wants his own business. _____

14. His small <u>family</u> looks to the future. _____

Using Adjectives: Complete the sentences. Write one adjective to describe each noun.

15. Maria strums the _____ guitar.

16. Lee beats the _____ drum.

17. Valerie listens to the _____ song.

18. Mac blows the _____ horn.

19. Thomas asks for the _____ tambourine.

20. Felicia whistles the _____ tune.

Master 6: Adjectives 2

Student's Name _____

An adjective is a word that describes a noun.

The adjectives are underlined. Each one describes a noun.

big city   old friend   one flag
honest man   red robin   pretty girl

Finding Adjectives: Circle the adjective that describes each underlined noun.

1. The beautiful <u>girl</u> loves to dance.

2. Mae reads difficult <u>books</u> about science.

3. The doctor worked in sunny <u>Los Angeles</u>.

4. Young <u>students</u> go to her camp.

5. The famous <u>woman</u> was born in Alabama.

6. She was an astronaut for six <u>years</u>.

7. She was the first <u>woman</u> of color in space.

Writing Adjectives: Read the adjectives. Write one to complete each sentence.

---

brave	visible	hottest	busy	amazing	small

---

8. The _____ astronaut floats in space.

9. The _____ scientist has many jobs.

10. He must pilot the _____ ship.

11. The _____ photograph shows the Earth.

12. The most _____ satellite is the Earth's moon.

13. Venus is the _____ planet of all.

Using Adjectives: Write an adjective to describe each noun.

14. _____ ocean   18. _____ fish

15. _____ mountain   19. _____ oars

16. _____ ship   20. _____ sailor

17. _____ water   21. _____ anchor

Master 7: Adverbs 1

Student's Name _____

An adverb is a word that describes a verb.

The adverbs are underlined. They describe a verb by telling how, when, and where.

How?	We worked <u>slowly</u>.
When?	We worked <u>today</u>.
Where?	They worked <u>nearby</u>.

Finding Adverbs: The verbs are underlined. Circle the adverbs that describe them.

1. Leon once <u>lived</u> in Germany.

2. He <u>studied</u> to be an actor here.

3. Yesterday he <u>acted</u> on TV in "Roots."

4. Gordy bravely <u>treks</u> to Africa.

5. Burton frequently <u>played</u> on game shows.

6. He quietly <u>enjoys</u> his many fans.

7. He <u>directs</u> other actors often.

8. The man <u>writes</u> music well.

9. He <u>speaks</u> gently to children.

Writing Adverbs: Write the adverbs. There is one in each sentence.

10. I watch the show closely. _____

11. I carefully study all the actors. _____

12. I often practice their lines. _____

13. I say them slowly in the mirror. _____

14. Then I shout the words wildly. _____

15. I sometimes try the stunts. _____

16. I foolishly attempted a fall. _____

17. My leg shattered badly below the knee. _____

18. Sign my cast there in big letters. _____

Using Adverbs: Complete each sentence with one adverb.

19. "Good morning," she said _____.

20. "Watch out," he said _____.

21. "Oops," she said _____.

22. "I told you so," he said _____.

Master 8: Adverbs 2

Student's Name _____

An adverb is a word that describes a verb.

The adverbs are underlined. They tell how, when, and where.

How?   Bake the bread <u>slowly</u>.

When?   Serve it <u>immediately</u>.

Where? Slice it <u>here</u>.

Finding Adverbs: Verbs are underlined. Circle the adverbs that describe them.

1. The man hastily <u>joined</u> the Navy.

2. Later, he <u>worked</u> as a law clerk.

3. Latimer <u>learned</u> about drafting easily.

4. He carefully <u>draws</u> a new invention.

5. He successfully <u>applied</u> for a patent.

6. His light bulb <u>shines</u> brightly.

7. People <u>use</u> it everywhere.

8. We <u>remember</u> his invention gratefully.

Writing Adverbs: Find the adverb in each sentence. Write it on the line.

9. Night falls earlier in the autumn. _____

10. The wind blows briskly through the trees. _____

11. I wrap a scarf snugly around my neck. _____

12. The leaves fall gently to the ground. _____

13. Then they swirl in the street. _____

14. We busily rake them into large bags. _____

15. Move the bags carefully to the curb. _____

Using Adverbs: Read the adverbs. Write one to complete each sentence.

usually	always	yesterday	today	rarely	never

16. He _____ raps.

17. She _____ hums.

18. He whistled _____ .

19. She bellowed _____ .

20. He _____ listens.

21. She _____ talks.

Master 9: Vocabulary Knowledge Rating Chart   Student's Name _____

1	2	3	4	5
Vocabulary Word	I know this word. I can explain its meaning and use it when I speak and write.	I think I know this word. It has something to do with _____.	I've seen or heard this word, but I'm not sure what it means.	I don't know this word. I need to learn it.

Master 10: Writing Rubric

Student's Name _____

	Focus	Organization	Conventions
4	Sentences are on the topic.	Sentences are very clear and use correct syntax. Word choice is good.	Sentences contain few, if any, errors in grammar, punctuation, capitalization, and/or spelling. Any errors that do occur do not get in the way of the reader's understanding.
3	Sentences are on the topic.	Sentences are mostly clear and use mostly correct syntax. Word choice is mostly good.	Sentences contain some errors in grammar, punctuation, capitalization, and/or spelling. These errors do not get in the way of the reader's understanding.
2	Sentences may be a bit off of the topic.	Sentences are sometimes difficult to follow. Words are sometimes misused.	Sentences contain several errors in grammar, punctuation, capitalization, and/or spelling. These errors may get in the way of the reader's understanding of the writing.
1	Sentences are not on the topic.	It is difficult for the reader to follow the writer's ideas. Words are often misused.	Sentences contain serious errors in grammar, punctuation, capitalization, and/or spelling. These errors make the writing very difficult for the reader to understand.

Master 11: Revising and Editing Checklist   Student's Name _____

When you **revise,** you add to or take away from your writing to make it clearer and more understandable. It always helps to read your work to a partner so that you can make sure it is well organized, includes enough details, and makes sense.

When you **edit,** look at the specific words you have chosen. Are they the best words? Check your work for proper spelling, punctuation, and usage. Make sure that you have not left out or repeated words. Have you used correct grammar?

Always revise before you edit. You don't want to spend time editing something you may not include in your revision.

Revising

_____ I read the sentences to myself to see if they made sense.

_____ I read the sentences to a partner to see if they made sense.

_____ My sentences stay on the topic.

_____ My sentences are logical and well organized.

Editing

_____ Each of my sentences ends with a period (.), a question mark (?), or an exclamation point (!).

_____ My subjects and verbs agree.

_____ I have used commas correctly.

_____ Each of my sentences begins with a capital letter.

_____ I have used quotation marks correctly.

_____ I chose my words carefully so that the reader can visualize just what I'm talking about.

_____ I inserted words that add interest to my sentences.

_____ I inserted words that were missing.

_____ I deleted extra words that I didn't need.

_____ I circled words that I think may be incorrectly spelled. I used additional resources to check the spelling of those words.

_____ I gave my edited sentences to a partner to check.

Master 12: Editor's Marks

Student's Name

Use these marks when editing your sentences. Make sure you understand what the marks mean when a teacher or partner uses them on your sentences.

Editing Marks		
≡	Changes a lowercase letter to an uppercase letter.	I visited kiwanis park with my cousins.
╱	Changes an uppercase letter to a lowercase letter.	Maria brought her Dog.
∧	Adds a word or punctuation mark.	We biked the park. _to_
_e_	Deletes a word or punctuation mark.	We ran around the the playground.
▭	Indicates incorrect word choice.	We had a lot of fun their _there_
⬭	Indicates a misspelled word.	We plan to go agin next weekend. _again_

Answers to Masters 1–8

MASTER 1: NOUNS 1

1. home, Alabama
2. Coretta, violin
3. couple, church
4. Martin, husband
5. India, month
6. People, hero
7. birthday, holiday
8. paper
9. soup
10. honey
11. hair
12. song
13. angle
14. cube
15. boxes
16.–20. Answers will vary.

MASTER 2: NOUNS 2

1. friends, park
2. chipmunk, path
3. children, playground
4. cars, street
5. Mothers, babies
6. people, office
7. family, fountain
8. pigeons
9. rooftops
10. pizza
11. Argentina
12. jungle
13. home
14.–18. Answers will vary.

MASTER 3: VERBS 1

1. race
2. begin
3. travel
4. pedals
5. steer
6. hops
7. respect
8. sags
9. jumps
10. leaps
11. stretches
12. kicks
13. reaches
14. sways, creaks
15. hear
16.–21. Answers will vary.

MASTER 4: VERBS 2

1. past
2. past
3. present
4. past
5. present
6. future
7. swings
8. will win
9. earned
10. breaks
11. defended
12. completes
13. race or will race
14. fill or will fill
15. pound or will pound
16. rumble or will rumble
17. rush or will rush

MASTER 5: ADJECTIVES 1

1. wet
2. tall
3. cool
4. good
5. blue
6. friendly
7. cozy
8. first
9. new
10. bright
11. tall
12. distant
13. proud
14. small
15.–20. Answers will vary.

MASTER 6: ADJECTIVES 2

1. beautiful
2. difficult
3. sunny
4. Young
5. famous
6. six
7. first
8. brave (or small)
9. busy
10. small (or amazing)
11. amazing (or small)
12. visible
13. hottest
14.–21. Answers will vary.

MASTER 7: ADVERBS 1

1. once
2. here
3. Yesterday
4. bravely
5. frequently
6. quietly
7. often
8. well
9. gently
10. closely
11. carefully
12. often
13. slowly
14. wildly
15. sometimes
16. foolishly
17. badly
18. there
19.–22. Answers will vary.

MASTER 8: ADVERBS 2

1. hastily
2. Later
3. easily
4. carefully
5. successfully
6. brightly
7. everywhere
8. gratefully
9. earlier
10. briskly
11. snugly
12. gently
13. Then
14. busily
15. carefully
16.–21. Answers will vary.